redefining
life: FORMEN

redefining
life: FOR**MEN**

A NAVSTUDY FEATURING THE**MESSAGE**®//REMIX™

Written and compiled by J. R. Briggs

TH1NK
P.O. Box 35001
Colorado Springs, Colorado 80935

www.navpress.com

TH1NK is an imprint of NavPress.

TH1NK and the TH1NK logo are registered trademarks of NavPress. Absence of ® in connection with marks of NavPress or other parties does not indicate an absence of registration of those marks.

ISBN 1-57683-987-7

Cover design by Kirk DouPonce, DogEaredDesign.com
Cover image by SuperStock
Creative Team: Nicci Hubert, Kathy Mosier, Arvid Wallen, Laura Spray

Written and compiled by J. R. Briggs

All Scripture quotations in this publication are taken from *THE MESSAGE* (MSG). Copyright © 1993, 1994, 1995, 1996, 2000, 2001, 2002. Used by permission of NavPress Publishing Group.

Printed in the United States of America

1 2 3 4 5 6 7 8 9 10 / 10 09 08 07 06

contents

about the redefininglife series

It's in Christ that we find out who we are and what we are living for.

Ephesians 1:11

For most of your life, you've been a student. And yet in a moment—probably marked by a ceremony—the title you carried for more than a dozen years was stripped away. So now how will you describe yourself when people ask? Are you a professional? An adult? A temporarily unemployed graduate? What seems to fit? Or do any of these fit at all?

Expectations are probably pretty high. But only a few of your graduating class fall into the life you wish you could have—the great job, the wonderful lifelong relationship, the incredible devotion to God. For the rest of you, it's back to square one in many ways. What has been defined for you in the past is suddenly up for negotiation.

The discussion guides in the REDEFINING LIFE series give you a forum to help with that negotiation process. They can help you figure out who you are, *who you really are*, whether you're still taking classes, employed full-time, or somewhere in between. They can help you find out what's really important in life, how to thrive in your work, and how to grow lifelong, meaningful relationships.

REDEFINING LIFE is a place to ask the hard questions of yourself and others. We're talking about a "marrow deep" kind of honesty. At the very least, these discussion guides will show you that you're not alone in the process of self-definition. And hopefully, they will also give you a glimpse—or maybe more—of God's role in the defining of you.

introduction

Keep your eyes open, hold tight to your convic-
tions, give it all you've got, be resolute, and
love without stopping.

1 Corinthians 16:13-14

We've all heard the line before. Maybe you heard it after you skinned your knee and started to cry. Or maybe you heard it when you faced an impending playground brawl at recess. No matter what the circumstance, most of us have heard the phrase before: "Be a man."

But what does it really mean to be a man? Can I show emotion? Can I interact deeply with other men? How do I treat women? Who defines what is "manly" and what isn't? And as a follower of Christ, how do I define myself as a guy? Am I man enough? These are difficult questions, the type that strike us at our deepest parts. They roll around in our brains and make us question ourselves at times. How we define manhood will have major implications on how we view life, how we behave, and how we treat others around us.

People often think that being a man and being a Christian are strange bedfellows. They think that Christian men can't have fun, be adventurous, cut loose, or be competitive and that, by nature, we somehow end up as wimpy, weak pushovers. Nowhere in Scripture does Jesus invite us into dull male lives. In fact, just the opposite. He desires for us as men to live life to its maximum potential, to squeeze every last drop out of life. To be men of our word. To strive to our deepest level. To pay attention. To live resolutely. And to constantly love with every fiber of our beings.

In this discussion guide, we will explore some key topics of what it means to be a real man, how to cultivate healthy relationships with male friends, how to have friendships with female friends, how to understand more of God as Father, and so on. We hope you will be able to wrestle with these questions head-on in a real, honest manner. We've designed this guide to the best of our ability with the hope that it's free of cheesy questions and trite answers but full of relevant and challenging questions that help you think critically about your everyday, Monday-morning life. The hope is that this forces you to deal with the question, "What does it mean for me to be a man who honors God in every area of my life?" As you work through this discussion guide, you'll begin to discover how to make healthy choices living life as a man of God.

how to use this discussion guide

REDEFINING LIFE isn't like any other study. We're not kidding. REDEFINING LIFE isn't designed with easy, obvious-to-answer questions and nice fill-in-the-blanks. It's got more of a wide-open-spaces feel to it.

The process is simple, really. Complete a lesson *on your own* (see details below). Then get with your small group and go through it again *together*. Got it?

Okay, want a little more direction than that? Here you go. And if you want even more help, check out the Discussion Group Study Tips (page 149) and the Frequently Asked Questions (page 151) sections in the back of the book.

1. Read, read, read. Each lesson contains five sections, but don't think of them as homework. This isn't an assignment to be graded. And at the end of the week, you don't have to turn it in to a teacher, professor, or boss. So don't read this as a "have to" but as a "get to." Think about how you read when you're on vacation. Set a leisurely pace. Try to enjoy what you read. Then read it again. Allow the words and meaning to soak in. Use the First Thoughts box to

> ## first thoughts
>
> like:
>
> dislike:
>
> agree:
>
> disagree:
>
> don't get it:

record your initial reactions to the text. (That's a sample on the previous page.) Then use the space provided in and around the reading to make notes. What bugs you? What inspires you? What doesn't make sense? What's confusing? Be honest. Be real. Be yourself. Don't shy away from phrases or sentences you don't understand or don't like. Circle them. Cross them out. Add exclamation marks or smiley faces.

2. Think about what you read. Think about what you wrote. Always ask:

- What does this mean?
- Why does this matter?
- How does this relate to my life right now?
- What does Scripture have to say about this?

Then respond to the questions provided. If you have a knack for asking questions, don't be shy about writing some of your own. You may have a lot to say on one topic, little on another. That's okay. When you come back to the passages in your small group, listen. Allow the experience of others to broaden your understanding and wisdom. You'll be stretched here — called on to evaluate what you've discovered and asked to make practical sense of it. In community, that stretching can often be painful and sometimes even embarrassing. But your willingness to be transparent — your openness to the possibility of personal growth — will reap great rewards. Vulnerability spurs growth in yourself and others.

3. Pray as you go through the entire session — before you begin reading, as you're thinking about a passage and its questions, and especially before you get together in a small group. Pause 'n' pray whenever you need to ask God for help along the way. Prayer takes many forms. You can speak your prayers. Be silent. Write them in the space at the bottom of each page. You can pray a Scripture or a spiritual song. Just don't forget that one of the most important parts of prayer is taking time to listen for God's response.

4. Live. What good are study, reflection, and prayer if they don't lead to action? When reflecting on the week's worth of lessons, think about what impacted you and how you can turn that lesson into action. After studying the issue of forgiveness, you may realize you need to write a letter or email to someone. After studying God's generosity, you may feel compelled to give a gift to a particular outreach. Figure out what God is calling you to do to live out your faith. Sometimes you'll finish a week's worth of lessons and each group member will decide to commit to the same goal. Other times you'll each walk away with a different conviction or goal. Record your goals in the book.

5. Follow up. What good are information and conversation if they don't lead to transformation? Your goal in doing any good study is to ultimately become more like Christ, and this is no exception. Prepare yourself to take your faith and make it active and alive. Be willing to set goals and hold others (as well as be held) accountable in your group. Part of being in a community of Jesus-followers means asking, "Hey, did you do what you said you were going to do?" It will help you put your faith into action as part of a community.

6. Repeat as necessary.

what makes a real man?

"In a word, what I'm saying is, *Grow up*. You're kingdom subjects. Now live like it. Live out your God-created identity."

Matthew 5:48

the defining line

We start every lesson by asking you to do a sometimes-difficult thing: define the core truths about the study topic as it relates to you right now. Use this "beginning place" to set the foundation for the lesson. You can then build, change, adjust, and otherwise redefine your life from there.

It doesn't take a rocket scientist or even a theologian to know that the world's definition of manhood and Scripture's definition of manhood are two completely different things. If you had to describe how the world defines what it means to be a man, what would you say? How (and who) is the model of manhood in our culture and why? Here's a harder question: How much of what is portrayed in the media and in our culture influences the way you believe you should act as a guy? Record your thoughts in the space below before reading further.

Now switch gears a bit. If you had to describe how Scripture defines what it means to be a man, how might you respond? How (and who) is the model of manhood found in the pages of your Bible? Why? And here's another thought to consider: How much of Scripture influences the way you consider what it means to be a guy? Record your thoughts below.

Be completely honest with yourself: If you were to look at your everyday life, which message influences your mindset on manhood the most? Is it what is portrayed through the media and society or through Scripture?

Consider sharing your responses with your group when you meet.

read The Sacrifices of Our Ordinary Living

Romans 12:1-2

So here's what I want you to do, God helping you: Take your everyday, ordinary life—your sleeping, eating, going-to-work, and walking-around life—and place it before God as an offering. Embracing what God does for you is the best thing you can do for him. Don't become so well-adjusted to your culture that you fit into it without even thinking. Instead, fix your attention on God. You'll be changed from the inside out. Readily recognize what he wants from you, and quickly respond to it. Unlike the culture around you, always dragging you down to its level of immaturity, God brings the best out of you, develops well-formed maturity in you.

---

first thoughts

like:

dislike:

agree:

disagree:

don't get it:

---

think

- How might this passage help us understand more of what it means to be a real man in the eyes of God? Be specific.
- Why do our ordinary life activities matter to God? To others?
- How does our culture say men should think, look, and act? How is this different from how God wants us to live? How are we to avoid becoming so well-adjusted to our culture that we fit in without thinking?
- How, practically, can you welcome God's efforts to make you a spiritually mature man?

pray

read Blatantly Honest

From *Searching for God Knows What* by Donald Miller[1]

Last year I caught an interview with Tom Arnold regarding his book *How I Lost Five Pounds in Six Years*. The interviewer asked why he had written the book, and I was somewhat amazed at the honesty of Arnold's answer. The comedian stated that most entertainers are in show business because they are broken people, looking for affirmation. "The reason I wrote this book," Tom Arnold said, "is because I wanted something out there so people would tell me they liked me. It's the reason behind almost everything I do." I have to tell you, after that, I really liked Tom Arnold. Leave it to an ex-alcoholic to tell the truth about life.

A few weeks later I was giving an interview in Seattle when the host asked me the same question of Tom Arnold: "Why did you write this book?" I wondered, on the air, if the explanation Tom Arnold gave was not the same reason I do what I do, and in the end I had to concede my motives of faith often take a backseat to my broken nature and desire to feel validity in life. I told the guy in Seattle that I am broken, that I like to write, but basically, subconsciously, I just want people to like me. The guy in Seattle leaned back in his chair, paused for a moment and said, "You aren't alone."

---

first thoughts

like:

dislike:

agree:

disagree:

don't get it:

---

think

- Think about Arnold's quote. How do you react to it?
- If you were interviewed about why you do certain things in life, how might your answer be similar to or different from Arnold's and Miller's? Why?
- Affirmation and validation aren't always a bad thing. When and why does our desire for affirmation and validation move from healthy to unhealthy?
- Can you think of times when your I-just-want-people-to-like-me desire has led you to make poor or damaging decisions?
- What does it mean to receive affirmation from God? How is that possible?

pray

read When We Feel Like Faking It (Part One)

From *TrueFaced: Trust God and Others with Who You Really Are* by Bill Thrall, Bruce McNicol, and John Lynch[2]

The ancient Greeks loved their theater. It was the Broadway of the Appian Way. But their immense outdoor amphitheaters had some built-in problems. People in the back row could not see the actors' faces, let alone their expressions. So some director came up with the idea of having the actors deliver their lines from behind giant masks.

All the actors held a pole that carried an enormous papier-mâché mask that portrayed their predominant nature—good or evil. The mask was always a caricature—an overdone, generalized, or idealized portrayal. If the playwright wanted to show that a character had changed during the play, that actor's mask was traded for another. But the actors never revealed their true faces. Throughout the play, they all acted out their roles behind a façade. These performers were not called actors, but hypocrites, literally, "one who wears a mask."[3] A hypocrite was one who continually wore masks and whose face the audience never saw.

A great mechanism for ancient Greek theater. A tragic mechanism for people who hunger to be known and loved in the light of day.

We are all performers, and like the actors in ancient Greece, we don't show our true faces. Because of sin, we've lost confidence that we will always please our audience, so we feel compelled to hide and put on a mask.

We have dozens of masks in our wardrobes, including:

- The "happy" mask
- The "I'm better than most" mask
- The "I'm very together" mask
- The "I'm a victim of others" mask
- The "I don't care" mask
- The "I am self-sufficient" mask
- The "I'm very important" mask
- The "I'm competent enough to not need love" mask

- The "I'm the expert" mask
- The "I am a theologically trained professional" mask
- The "I'm not hurt" mask
- The "I have the answers" mask
- The "I am independent" mask
- The "I am cool" mask

---

first thoughts

like:

dislike:

agree:

disagree:

don't get it:

---

think

- In what situations is it easiest for you to wear a mask? Be specific.
- The authors describe the Greek actor's mask as "an overdone, generalized, or idealized portrayal." Take off your masks right now, even if for a minute, and honestly answer this question: Have you portrayed yourself to others as overdone, generalized, and/or idealized? How?
- Look at the list of masks. Which mask is the most tempting for you to reach for? If your best friend, mom or dad, roommate, or girlfriend/wife were to answer this question about you, which one might they pick?
- What masks are most useful to men? Why?
- How wide is the gap between how others perceive you and your true self? Is this healthy or unhealthy? What can be done to narrow the gap?
- What does this ultimately do to our true identity?

pray

read When You Feel Like Faking It
(Part Two)

From *Hamlet* by William Shakespeare

God hath given you one face, and you make yourselves another.

From "Façade" from the musical *Jekyll and Hyde*

There is a face that we hide
Till the nighttime appears,
And what's hiding inside,
Behind all of our fears,
Is our true self
Locked inside the façade!

From *Macbeth* by William Shakespeare

Away, and mock the time with fairest show;
False face must hide what the false heart doth know.

Luke 12:1-2

"Watch yourselves carefully so you don't get contaminated with Pharisee yeast, Pharisee phoniness. You can't keep your true self hidden forever; before long you'll be exposed. You can't hide behind a religious mask forever; sooner or later the mask will slip and your true face will be known."

first thoughts

like:

dislike:

agree:

disagree:

don't get it:

think

- What common threads do you see in these quotes?
- Why are these themes important to note? How are they relevant to you?
- Why is it alluring to pretend we are somebody we are not? How does this damage our identity and self-esteem?
- How does fear contribute to our masks?
- Think about the first Shakespeare quote. Why are we often displeased with the "one face" God has given us, and why do we work so hard to make ourselves a different one?

pray

read Human Beings Versus Human Doings

Philippians 3:3-11

The *real* believers are the ones the Spirit of God leads to work away at this ministry, filling the air with Christ's praise as we do it. We couldn't carry this off by our own efforts, and we know it — even though we can list what many might think are impressive credentials. You know my pedigree: a legitimate birth, circumcised on the eighth day; an Israelite from the elite tribe of Benjamin; a strict and devout adherent to God's law; a fiery defender of the purity of my religion, even to the point of persecuting the church; a meticulous observer of everything set down in God's law Book.

The very credentials these people are waving around as something special, I'm tearing up and throwing out with the trash — along with everything else I used to take credit for. And why? Because of Christ. Yes, all the things I once thought were so important are gone from my life. Compared to the high privilege of knowing Christ Jesus as my Master, firsthand, everything I once thought I had going for me is insignificant — dog dung. I've dumped it all in the trash so that I could embrace Christ and be embraced by him. I didn't want some petty, inferior brand of righteousness that comes from keeping a list of rules when I could get the robust kind that comes from trusting Christ — *God's* righteousness.

I gave up all that inferior stuff so I could know Christ personally, experience his resurrection power, be a partner in his suffering, and go all the way with him to death itself. If there was any way to get in on the resurrection from the dead, I wanted to do it.

---

first thoughts

like:

dislike:

agree:

disagree:

don't get it:

---

think

- As men, it's so easy to find our identity in our accomplishments and titles. Why is this the case? Why might it be an unhealthy approach to finding our true self-worth and identity as men?
- Paul claims that his identity does not come from what he has accomplished. What is he staking his confidence on, and how does that change his perspective?
- If you were to ask your friends where they think you get your self-esteem and identity, what might they say? How much of that would revolve around your job or your academic or professional successes or failures? Why?
- How different would our lives be if we were able to define ourselves not by what we accomplish but by who we belong to?
- How would our mindsets have to change in order for this to happen?
- What areas of our lives would we need to release?

pray

live The Redefining

Take a few moments to skim through the notes you've made in these readings. What do they tell you about what God desires from you as a man? Based on what you've read and discussed, is there anything you want to change?

What, if anything, is stopping you from making this change?

How has your perspective of what it means to be a man of God changed, modified, or solidified from what you've read this week?

What is the biggest obstacle keeping you from being the man you believe God desires you to be in the coming weeks, months, and years?

Talk with a close friend about all of the above. Brainstorm together about what it might take to move toward God in this area of your life. Determine what this looks like in a practical sense and then list any measurable goals you want to shoot for here. Review these goals each week to see how you are doing.

who's your daddy?

"Live out this God-created identity the way our Father lives toward us, generously and graciously, even when we're at our worst. Our Father is kind; you be kind."

Luke 6:35-36

a reminder

Before you dive into this next study, spend a little time reviewing what you wrote in the previous lesson's Live section. How are you doing? Check with your small-group members and review your progress toward the specific goals. If necessary, adjust your goals and plans and then recommit to them.

the defining line

For better or worse, our experiences with our earthly fathers will directly impact our concept of God as our heavenly Father. Maybe to you, God as Father is a cruel tyrant, someone you could never impress no matter how hard you tried. Or maybe this idea evokes wonderful thoughts of friendship and wisdom and guidance that He provides.

Jesus' earthly father, Joseph, was instrumental in shaping the mind of Jesus to understand His heavenly Father. I have often wondered to what extent his influence, actions, language, and love affected young Jesus as He was growing up. Joseph modeled the very love and obedience that God the Father asks of each one of us.

How we view God as our Father will have a huge impact on how we live and pray and worship and love. Understanding the heart of our Father God is of utmost importance to us as men. If we can grasp the role of the loving heavenly Father, then we can begin to live in our role as His children, as His sons. And this, in turn, will help many of us, who will one day become fathers to our sons and will have a chance to shape in them a healthy understanding of what it means for God to be *their* Father.

It has been said that we live in a fatherless generation. If you were to reflect on your relationship with your father, what would come to mind? Would your heart break? Are you bitter because you have had a less-than-beneficial experience with your dad? Or would you rejoice because you have been fortunate enough to maintain a great relationship with him?

Consider sharing your responses with your group when you meet.

read Talking with Dad

Matthew 6:7-13

"The world is full of so-called prayer warriors who are prayer-ignorant. They're full of formulas and programs and advice, peddling techniques for getting what you want from God. Don't fall for that nonsense. This is your Father you are dealing with, and he knows better than you what you need. With a God like this loving you, you can pray very simply. Like this:

> Our Father in heaven,
> Reveal who you are.
> Set the world right;
> Do what's best—
>   as above, so below.
> Keep us alive with three square meals.
> Keep us forgiven with you and forgiving others.
> Keep us safe from ourselves and the Devil.
> You're in charge!
> You can do anything you want!
> You're ablaze in beauty!
>   Yes. Yes. Yes."

Galatians 4:4-7

But when the time arrived that was set by God the Father, God sent his Son, born among us of a woman, born under the conditions of the law so that he might redeem those of us who have been kidnapped by the law. Thus we have been set free to experience our rightful heritage. You can tell for sure that you are now fully adopted as his own children because God sent the Spirit of his Son into our lives crying out, "Papa! Father!" Doesn't that privilege of intimate conversation with God make it plain that you are not a slave, but a child? And if you are a child, you're also an heir, with complete access to the inheritance.

James 1:5

If you don't know what you're doing, pray to the Father. He loves to help. You'll get his help, and won't be condescended to when you ask for it.

---

first thoughts

like:

dislike:

agree:

disagree:

don't get it:

---

think

- How does the fact that God knows better what you need than you do influence or alter the way you pray? Does it make you want to pray more or less? Why?
- Does addressing God as "our Father" in prayer come easily to you, or is it difficult? Why?
- Most of the time, do you see "intimate conversation" as a privilege or a duty? Why?
- Why do you think it's so hard for many of us to grasp the fact that God our Father loves us so much and wants to hear us and help us?

- To what degree does our understanding of God as our Father affect the way we pray and how often we talk to Him?

pray

read Indescribable Love

Luke 15:11-32

Then he said, "There was once a man who had two sons. The younger said to his father, 'Father, I want right now what's coming to me.'

"So the father divided the property between them. It wasn't long before the younger son packed his bags and left for a distant country. There, undisciplined and dissipated, he wasted everything he had. After he had gone through all his money, there was a bad famine all through that country and he began to hurt. He signed on with a citizen there who assigned him to his fields to slop the pigs. He was so hungry he would have eaten the corncobs in the pig slop, but no one would give him any.

"That brought him to his senses. He said, 'All those farmhands working for my father sit down to three meals a day, and here I am starving to death. I'm going back to my father. I'll say to him, Father, I've sinned against God, I've sinned before you; I don't deserve to be called your son. Take me on as a hired hand.' He got right up and went home to his father.

"When he was still a long way off, his father saw him. His heart pounding, he ran out, embraced him, and kissed him. The son started his speech: 'Father, I've sinned against God, I've sinned before you; I don't deserve to be called your son ever again.'

"But the father wasn't listening. He was calling to the servants, 'Quick. Bring a clean set of clothes and dress him. Put the family ring on his finger and sandals on his feet. Then get a grain-fed heifer and roast it. We're going to feast! We're going to have a wonderful time! My son is here—given up for dead and now alive! Given up for lost and now found!' And they began to have a wonderful time.

"All this time his older son was out in the field. When the day's work was done he came in. As he approached the house, he heard the music and dancing. Calling over one of the houseboys, he asked what was going on. He told him, 'Your brother came home. Your father has ordered a feast—barbecued beef!—because he has him home safe and sound.'

"The older brother stalked off in an angry sulk and refused to join in. His father came out and tried to talk to him, but he wouldn't listen. The son said, 'Look how many years I've stayed here serving you, never giving you one moment of grief, but have you ever thrown a party for me and my friends? Then this son of yours who has thrown away your money on whores shows up and you go all out with a feast!'

"His father said, 'Son, you don't understand. You're with me all the time, and everything that is mine is yours—but this is a wonderful time, and we had to celebrate. This brother of yours was dead, and he's alive! He was lost, and he's found!'"

---

first thoughts

like:

dislike:

agree:

disagree:

don't get it:

---

think

- Is it easy for you to imagine that God loves you in the same way as the father in this story? Why or why not?
- Think about the two different ways the father dealt with his sons. Can you think of times in your life when you've acted like the

younger son and the older son? How has God dealt with you in those situations?

- What are the advantages of a Father God who loves you in the same manner as the father in this story?
- Does it take a lot of effort to visualize that God is a Father who loves to celebrate? Why or why not?

pray

read Faith of Our Fathers

From "Healing 'Father Wounds'" by Ted Roberts[1]

The muscular young man poured out his soul to me as I sat listening intently. The frustrations and hurts cascaded out of his heart as tears streamed down his face.

Through the years, I have listened to the hearts of hundreds of hurting men like him. The painful refrain is usually about what they wish their dads had said to them. Now they may not phrase it this way, but it's obvious that they are struggling with a deep "father wound."

There are three things we should know that every son wants to hear from his father. First, he needs to hear his dad say, "I believe in you, Son." . . .

The second thing every son needs to hear is, "I'm sorry." Not so the son can say, "I'm right." But so the son can say, "I'm sorry too, Dad."

There are no perfect father-child relationships; we all need to be forgiven. Our heavenly Father always moves passionately toward us. That is why we will only understand who we are and who we truly can become as we discover over and over again that we are beloved of God.

I love the prayer, "Father, help me to understand what You had in mind when You made the original me." It is in the embrace of Father God that we finally find out who we really are.

The third thing that men cry to hear from their fathers is, "I love you." . . .

Sure, disobedience has consequences, but God will still love me. Whenever a man comes to truly know his heavenly Father, he will be constantly saying to his kids: "I believe in you. I am

first thoughts
like:
dislike:
agree:
disagree:
don't get it:

sorry. I love you." Because that is what he hears his heavenly Father saying to him.

think

- How has your relationship with your father influenced your understanding of God?
- As men, there are three statements we long to hear from our fathers: "I believe in you," "I'm sorry," and "I love you." Have you heard those words from your father? Why are they so important?
- We know God is perfect, so He has no need to say He's sorry. But have you felt God saying to you that He believes in you and that He loves you?
- Someday (if you haven't already) you might become a father. What are some of your goals for fatherhood?

pray

read Keeping Company

1 John 3:1

What marvelous love the Father has extended to us! Just look at it—we're called children of God! That's who we really are.

John 8:19-39

They said, "Where is this so-called Father of yours?"

Jesus said, "You're looking right at me and you don't see me. How do you expect to see the Father? If you knew me, you would at the same time know the Father."

He gave this speech in the Treasury while teaching in the Temple. No one arrested him because his time wasn't yet up.

Then he went over the same ground again. "I'm leaving and you are going to look for me, but you're missing God in this and are headed for a dead end. There is no way you can come with me."

The Jews said, "So, is he going to kill himself? Is that what he means by 'You can't come with me'?"

Jesus said, "You're tied down to the mundane; I'm in touch with what is beyond your horizons. You live in terms of what you see and touch. I'm living on other terms. I told you that you were missing God in all this. You're at a dead end. If you won't believe I am who I say I am, you're at the dead end of sins. You're missing God in your lives."

They said to him, "Just who are you anyway?"

Jesus said, "What I've said from the start. I have so many things to say that concern you, judgments to make that affect you, but if you don't accept the trustworthiness of the One who commanded my words and acts, none of it matters. That is who you are questioning—not me but the One who sent me."

They still didn't get it, didn't realize that he was referring to the Father. So Jesus tried again. "When you raise up the Son of Man, then you will know who I am—that I'm not making this up, but speaking only what the Father taught me. The One who sent me stays with me. He doesn't abandon me. He sees how much joy I take in pleasing him."

When he put it in these terms, many people decided to believe.

Then Jesus turned to the Jews who had claimed to believe in him. "If you stick with this, living out what I tell you, you are my disciples for sure. Then you will experience for yourselves the truth, and the truth will free you."

Surprised, they said, "But we're descendants of Abraham. We've never been slaves to anyone. How can you say, 'The truth will free you'?"

Jesus said, "I tell you most solemnly that anyone who chooses a life of sin is trapped in a dead-end life and is, in fact, a slave. A slave is a transient, who can't come and go at will. The Son, though, has an established position, the run of the house. So if the Son sets you free, you are free through and through. I know you are Abraham's descendants. But I also know that you are trying to kill me because my message hasn't yet penetrated your thick skulls. I'm talking about things I have seen while keeping company with the Father, and you just go on doing what you have heard from your father."

They were indignant. "Our father is Abraham!"

Jesus said, "If you were Abraham's children, you would have been doing the things Abraham did."

---

first thoughts

like:

dislike:

agree:

disagree:

don't get it:

---

think

- Why did Jesus make such a close correlation between Himself and God the Father? Why do you think the religious people Jesus addressed didn't get it?

- Jesus describes things He has seen "while keeping company with the Father." Why is it important for us to keep company with the Father? What impact should that have on our lives specifically and practically, on a daily basis?

- What distinction does Jesus draw between "your father" and the Father in verse 38?

- What are some ways in which you can keep company with your heavenly Father on a more consistent basis?

pray

read The Image of the Father

From "Hallowed Be Thy Name: Image of God as Father Is Declining" by Kenneth L. Woodward[2]

God as a father is no longer a popular concept in modern religion. He is more often referred to as a king or lord without reference to being father to his worshippers. Jesus and Mary seem to be more popular in the Christian religion than God as a figure of worship.

These are tough times to be a father. The media are full of stories about abusive fathers, fatherless children and deadbeat dads—and about New Fathers who are trying to do better. But in general this is an age when fathers get little respect, and you don't have to look farther than the biggest father figure of them all, God.

Consider: fundamentalist and evangelical Christians fixate on God's son. It is Jesus who must be experienced if you are to be saved. Pentecostal Christians cherish the power of the Holy Spirit. When Catholics look for a model of Christian perfection, they find it in Mary. In their determination to be "inclusive," many mainline Protestants are busily excising all mention of a paternal deity from hymns and prayer books. New Age Jews are edging toward the use of "Yah" for the ineffable name of the Lord, partly as an effort to wipe out any lingering association with the masculine gender. Only among the Mormons, who believe that all humans were begotten in heaven as God's own "spirit children," is the Father recognized for his paternity. How can God the Father compete with a divine Son, a perfect Virgin Mother and the anti-patriarchal Spirit of the Times?

Even the Scriptures are cool to God as Father. In the Hebrew Bible, God is most often addressed as "the Holy One," "King" or "Lord." Except in some of the Psalms, he is rarely referred to as "Father." An observation from the Jerusalem Talmud puts it wryly. Why is it, one rabbi asks, that "when Israel is not in trouble, [the Israelites] do not say, 'Thou art our father.' But only when they come into trouble do they seek Thee."

Jesus, of course, addressed all his prayers to his heavenly "Father" and taught his disciples to do the same. He even called him "Abba," a term of intimacy that means something like "daddy" in Aramaic. But as an essayist pointed out more than 20 years ago in *The American Scholar*, the New Testament (like most Western literature) is written from the son's point of view. It is his story that is told, his divinity that is celebrated. In Christian art, it is Jesus and his mother who are most often depicted. When the Father is shown at all, he almost always shares the scene with Jesus and the Holy Spirit, the other figures of the Trinity. Early Christians saw him as a young man, much like his son; later Christian art reduced his presence to a single hand reaching down from a cloud, and by the 15th century he had become a bearded old man, sometimes outfitted like a Renaissance pope. Michelangelo's powerful Creator on the Sistine Chapel ceiling is a singular image of a vigorous God the Father, but one that feminists like Sister Elizabeth Johnson, president of the Catholic Theological Society of America, find all too "androcentric" for contemporary sensibilities.

Jesus enjoined his followers to "be perfect, just as your heavenly Father is perfect." But in any religious scheme, it is hard to imagine the creator of the universe as paterfamilias. To Muslims, Allah is the all-powerful and the all-merciful, but "Father" is not among his 99 names. In the complex family systems of Hindu gods and goddesses, Brahma is the creator. But in all of India, there is only a handful of temples in his name, whereas the sonlike avatars Vishnu, Krishna and Rama have thousands of temples devoted to their worship. In Buddhism, there is no creator. But it is noteworthy that in the story of the Buddha, Prince Siddhartha deserts his wife before he attains enlightenment.

first thoughts

like:

dislike:

agree:

disagree:

don't get it:

think

- "God as a father is no longer a popular concept in modern religion." Do you agree with this statement? Why or why not?
- Why is it significant that Christianity is the only major religion that deals with God as a Father figure?
- Why does our concept of God as Father matter to Christians?
- How does understanding God as our loving Father impact times of suffering?

pray

live The Redefining

Take a few moments to skim through the notes you've made in these readings. What do they tell you about God as our Father? Based on what you've read and discussed, is there anything that you want to change? Describe this below.

What, if anything, is stopping you from making this change?

What can you be doing in the next several weeks to become more acquainted with your heavenly Father? Be specific.

Is it hard for you to accept the fact that your heavenly Father is loving and caring? How is this related to your own relationship with your earthly father? Tell God your thoughts in prayer right now.

Talk with a close friend about all of the above. Brainstorm together about what it might take to move toward God in this area of your life. Determine what this looks like in a practical sense and then list any measurable goals you want to shoot for here. Review these goals each week to see how you are doing.

testing
ground

Don't be so naive and self-confident. You're not exempt. You could fall flat on your face as easily as anybody else. Forget about self-confidence; it's useless. Cultivate God-confidence. No test or temptation that comes your way is beyond the course of what others have had to face. All you need to remember is that God will never let you down; he'll never let you be pushed past your limit; he'll always be there to help you come through it.

1 Corinthians 10:12-13

a reminder

Before you dive into this study, spend a little time reviewing what you wrote in the previous lessons' Live sections. How are you doing? Check with your small-group members and review your progress toward the specified goals. If necessary, adjust your goals and plans and then recommit to them.

the defining line

Temptation, especially sexual temptation, seems to be one of the most difficult, if not the most difficult, areas in our Christian life as guys. Movies, magazines, websites, advertisements, billboards, sporting events, commercials.

Temptation is everywhere and at times can seem hard to avoid, no matter what we do. But temptation can include other areas as well: pride, power, recognition from others, money, fame. The list goes on and on. And it seems to pop up when we're most vulnerable and susceptible.

Temptation forces us to make a conscious decision: to do the right thing or to fall to the enticing and attractive areas of sin. On paper it makes sense, but when we find ourselves in those specific situations, it can seem like the hardest thing in the whole world to not give in.

Think back to a time in the past several weeks or months when you fell to temptation. What happened?

Now think back to a time in the past several weeks or months when you were able to resist temptation. How were you able to resist it?

Consider sharing your responses with your group when you meet.

read A Killer

James 1:12-18

Anyone who meets a testing challenge head-on and manages to stick it out is mighty fortunate. For such persons loyally in love with God, the reward is life and more life.

Don't let anyone under pressure to give in to evil say, "God is trying to trip me up." God is impervious to evil, and puts evil in no one's way. The temptation to give in to evil comes from us and only us. We have no one to blame but the leering, seducing flare-up of our own lust. Lust gets pregnant, and has a baby: sin! Sin grows up to adulthood, and becomes a real killer.

So, my very dear friends, don't get thrown off course. Every desirable and beneficial gift comes out of heaven. The gifts are rivers of light cascading down from the Father of Light. There is nothing deceitful in God, nothing two-faced, nothing fickle. He brought us to life using the true Word, showing us off as the crown of all his creatures.

---

first thoughts

like:

dislike:

agree:

disagree:

don't get it:

---

think

- Think about your most common struggles with sin. When are you most likely to give in to these sins? Why?
- Think about the analogy James uses to describe the life cycle of sin: "Lust gets pregnant, and has a baby: sin! Sin grows up to adulthood, and becomes a real killer." Have you seen that in your life? Based on your experiences, what are some ways you can avoid "pregnancy" from the beginning?
- Do you find it is easy to blame God when you have fallen into sin?
- Think about your upcoming week. What implications does this passage have for you in the next few days? How does the passage influence your interaction and relationships with other guys?

pray

read Temptation Island

From "I Am Trapped," author anonymous[1]

I'm trapped. And it's nobody's fault but my own.

I guarantee you've met me, or at least someone like me. Maybe you don't know it, but 20 minutes after you see me at the church, I'm at my computer. And I'm in a world you probably thought couldn't touch me.

Never before have I felt so much like Paul, while feeling so little like a disciple. I can relate to the apostle's words: "What I don't understand about myself is that I decide one way, and then act another, doing things I absolutely despise" (Romans 7:15, *The Message*).

Now, I don't know whether or not Paul ever had DSL at his house. I do know, however, that when he referred to himself as the "foremost" of sinners, he didn't see me coming. How your worship pastor could get caught up in all of this, you may never understand. But here I am, drowning in pornography, unable (unwilling?) to climb out.

It seems simple enough. I've counseled people on this very issue, simply defining the steps to my victory over porn in my high school years. "Spend time in the Word," I'd say. "Find an accountability partner," I'd say. "Get rid of whatever it is that is allowing you to stumble," I'd say. But even in those instances, I never felt far enough removed from my own temptations to be comfortable in advising the ones who were coming to me for guidance.

I stayed away from the stuff for years. Through college, marriage, kids and ministry, I was able to ignore the tug of the thoughts still embedded in my mind from my very first experiences with pornographic material. I didn't watch rated "R" movies. Stayed away from HBO and Showtime after 8 p.m. *Glamour* magazine? Sorry, George Costanza. I'm not falling into that trap.

I don't know the exact date (although I'm sure I could find it here on my hard drive somewhere), but a day came when temptation came around the corner and hit me square between the eyes. That was it. I didn't see him coming, but Satan's been sitting on my lap for the past two months.

That's nine Sundays. Twenty-seven worship services. Forty-five days in the office, about 2,000 handshakes, 400 hugs, 135 praise choruses and two baptisms—all of it with a heart that isn't prepared to worship the Lord, let alone lead others to Him. And it's affecting my ministry. I'm losing volunteers. I'm getting in arguments with staff members. I've lied to the congregation. It's gotten to the point where I hate going to work. And you know what I hate even worse? That I now refer to it as "work."

I remember counseling a kid who had been using file-sharing software to download x-rated videos on his parents' computer. He could send the stuff to a folder that his parents didn't know existed, he never had to visit a website so there was no history to clean up, and all he had to do to get it in the first place was type in a search phrase, and thousands of files would pop up for his viewing pleasure.

Now his game is mine. I find myself sitting at the computer, typing into a search engine the kinds of words I don't even say. I get the files in a matter of seconds, and there's hardly any cleanup to hide my adulterous behavior from my wife. That doesn't keep me, mind you, from spending nearly every waking minute worrying I've missed one of my tracks, and that my marriage, my ministry, my life will be over at any minute.

So why don't I listen to all the things "I said" to other people and take my own advice? Good question. I should get into the Word, and stay there for about two weeks straight, but I can't open my Bible without breaking out in tears of guilt and feelings of worthlessness. Get rid of the Internet connection? Explain to the staff why I'm not getting their emails. Find an accountability partner? If you can suggest one, I'm open to your thoughts. My pastor? Sure. But, lest you forget, he can fire me. The Elders? See previous comment.

Okay. I heard you out there under your breath (the ones who said "well, you should be fired"). Don't think for one second that I don't agree. If you want to know the truth, I truly want to resign. I want to let my peers and my pastor know that I've let them down and I've let God down. I want to take time to step away and make this right. Problem is, I don't have the nerve. If you sat down at my dinner table with my wife and kids looking you in the face, you probably wouldn't either.

Speaking of that lovely family, how do you say to your wife, "Honey, I've sinned against you and the kids. Can we drop the broadband?" She's been nothing but loving and faithful to me, and I'm getting my kicks from some poor girl in the San Fernando Valley.

If there's one thing I know, it's that I need out of this, and now. I'm certainly not there at this moment. If you're interested, it's been about an hour and a half since I last checked to see if there was anything good available through my favorite file-sharing program. I'm a saved man making a mockery of the cross. It's breaking my heart, and I feel like I'm the most worthless creature God has made. I'm risking harming my family and my congregation because of my stupid flesh.

I know that some will be quick to judge me, and that's okay. I would certainly hope that the majority of you reading this are doing better in your walk than I. But whatever your opinion of me, know that 37 percent of America's pastors struggle with a pornography addiction on a daily basis. I'm not alone—not that I take comfort in that, nor should any of the rest of you who are caught up in this mess. Our only comfort is in a God who can pull us out of this crap.

And so, in front of all of you, I'm throwing out this prayer:

Dear God,

Help.

[The author of this article is a worship pastor for a growing Midwestern church and wishes to remain anonymous. He asks for your prayers.]

---

first thoughts

like:

dislike:

agree:

disagree:

don't get it:

---

think

- The author suggested that readers who desire to leave pornography behind should spend time in the Word, find an accountability partner, and get rid of whatever it is that allows them to stumble. Are his suggestions helpful? Why or why not?
- For various reasons, the author feels he can't share his addiction with others. If this is a struggle for you, what keeps you from sharing it with others? Why?
- The author has requested to remain anonymous. If this were your situation and you had written this article, would you have stayed anonymous or given your name? Why?
- What are the benefits of sharing sins and temptations with others? What are the drawbacks? Is it worth sharing with others?

pray

read "Sleep with Me"

Genesis 39:1-12

After Joseph had been taken to Egypt by the Ishmaelites, Potiphar an Egyptian, one of Pharaoh's officials and the manager of his household, bought him from them.

As it turned out, GOD was with Joseph and things went very well with him. He ended up living in the home of his Egyptian master. His master recognized that GOD was with him, saw that GOD was working for good in everything he did. He became very fond of Joseph and made him his personal aide. He put him in charge of all his personal affairs, turning everything over to him. From that moment on, GOD blessed the home of the Egyptian—all because of Joseph. The blessing of GOD spread over everything he owned, at home and in the fields, and all Potiphar had to concern himself with was eating three meals a day.

Joseph was a strikingly handsome man. As time went on, his master's wife became infatuated with Joseph and one day said, "Sleep with me."

He wouldn't do it. He said to his master's wife, "Look, with me here, my master doesn't give a second thought to anything that goes on here—he's put me in charge of everything he owns. He treats me as an equal. The only thing he hasn't turned over to me is you. You're his wife, after all! How could I violate his trust and sin against God?"

She pestered him day after day after day, but he stood his ground. He refused to go to bed with her.

On one of these days he came to the house to do his work

first thoughts

like:

dislike:

agree:

disagree:

don't get it:

and none of the household servants happened to be there. She grabbed him by his cloak, saying, "Sleep with me!" He left his coat in her hand and ran out of the house.

think

- Like Joseph, do you ever feel like temptation pesters you day after day after day?
- How do you think Joseph stood his ground despite enduring constant temptation over a long period of time?
- Notice that Joseph didn't walk out of the house when Potiphar's wife grabbed him by his cloak. It says that he ran. What does it mean for you to run out of the house of temptation in your daily life?
- To what extent do you think Joseph might have felt tempted to cave in and sleep with Potiphar's wife?
- What can we learn from Joseph when it comes to dealing with sexual sin in our own lives, especially when it seems to be all around us in our culture?

pray

read Out of Trouble

From "Take It from Me: Ben Roethlisberger: Steelers QB Ben Roethlisberger Shows You How to Launch Your Own Winning Streak," an interview with Jim Thornton[2]

I'm surrounded by temptations. I've had women ask me to sign every conceivable body part. They send me bras and underwear to autograph. I've never signed any of it. All of us are sinners, and everyone screws up sometimes. Still, I attempt to always remember what's right and wrong. As an NFL player, you can't always stay out of the media, but you can stay out of trouble. You can also practice good sportsmanship. Being a nice guy doesn't make you any less of a competitor.

---

first thoughts

like:

dislike:

agree:

disagree:

don't get it:

---

think

- What temptations surround you at work and school and in your friendships, home life, and personal life?
- What does it mean to stay out of trouble, even when nobody is looking or it seems that everyone is condoning inappropriate behavior?
- Honestly, if you were in Ben's situation as a star quarterback, how might you handle temptation?
- What are some ways we can attempt to always remember what's right and what's wrong?

pray

read The Test

Matthew 4:1-11

Next Jesus was taken into the wild by the Spirit for the Test. The Devil was ready to give it. Jesus prepared for the Test by fasting forty days and forty nights. That left him, of course, in a state of extreme hunger, which the Devil took advantage of in the first test: "Since you are God's Son, speak the word that will turn these stones into loaves of bread."

Jesus answered by quoting Deuteronomy: "It takes more than bread to stay alive. It takes a steady stream of words from God's mouth."

For the second test the Devil took him to the Holy City. He sat him on top of the Temple and said, "Since you are God's Son, jump." The Devil goaded him by quoting Psalm 91: "He has placed you in the care of angels. They will catch you so that you won't so much as stub your toe on a stone."

Jesus countered with another citation from Deuteronomy: "Don't you dare test the Lord your God."

For the third test, the Devil took him on the peak of a huge mountain. He gestured expansively, pointing out all the earth's kingdoms, how glorious they all were. Then he said, "They're yours—lock, stock, and barrel. Just go down on your knees and worship me, and they're yours."

Jesus' refusal was curt: "Beat it, Satan!" He backed his rebuke with a third quotation from Deuteronomy: "Worship the Lord your God, and only him. Serve him with absolute single-heartedness."

The Test was over. The Devil left. And in his place, angels! Angels came and took care of Jesus' needs.

---

first thoughts

like:

dislike:

agree:

disagree:

don't get it:

---

think

- Jesus was tempted in three main areas: power, potential, and praise. How do you find that you are tempted in these areas? Be specific.
- Jesus combated temptation by using Scripture as His basis for defense. How do you combat temptation? Has Satan ever used Scripture to convince you to sin? Have you ever done this yourself? When and how?
- Satan tempted Jesus by quoting Scripture but taking it out of context and altering the truth a little. How do you see temptation sprout up in your life through truth that has been altered?
- Satan has a way of tempting us with enticing things when we are at our weakest. Why is that? What are some specific principles we can learn from Jesus through His interaction with the Devil?

pray

live   The Redefining

Take a few moments to skim through the notes you've made in these readings. What do they tell you about avoiding temptation? Based on what you've read and discussed, is there anything that you want to change? Describe this below.

What, if anything, is stopping you from making this change?

What are some specific ways you can create barriers to temptation in your own life that will help you resist sin?

Who are some male friends you can confide in when it comes to sharing your struggles and being held accountable in situations of temptation?

Talk with a close friend about all of the above. Brainstorm together about what it might take to move toward God in this area of your life. Determine what this looks like in a practical sense and then list any measurable goals you want to shoot for here. Review these goals each week to see how you are doing.

the leading
edge

Love and truth form a good leader;
      sound leadership is founded on loving integrity.

Proverbs 20:28

a reminder

Before you dive into this study, spend a little time reviewing what you wrote in the previous lessons' Live sections. How are you doing? Check with your small-group members and review your progress toward the specified goals. If necessary, adjust your goals and plans and then recommit to them.

the defining line

Most people in the business world would say that companies will rise and fall on leadership. The same is true for our lives in the spiritual realm. Most of the time, the difference between good and bad leadership is significant. And the world is starving for good, honest, and confident yet humble leaders.

Think about the leaders you know. Can you name two or three men who have been models of godly leadership for you?

If three or four of your closest friends gathered to describe you as a leader (and you weren't in the room), what might they say about you? What makes you think this?

Consider sharing your responses with your group when you meet.

read Fit to Lead

1 Timothy 3:1-7

If anyone wants to provide leadership in the church, good! But there are preconditions: A leader must be well-thought-of, committed to his wife, cool and collected, accessible, and hospitable. He must know what he's talking about, not be overfond of wine, not pushy but gentle, not thin-skinned, not money-hungry. He must handle his own affairs well, attentive to his own children and having their respect. For if someone is unable to handle his own affairs, how can he take care of God's church? He must not be a new believer, lest the position go to his head and the Devil trip him up. Outsiders must think well of him, or else the Devil will figure out a way to lure him into his trap.

---

first thoughts

like:

dislike:

agree:

disagree:

don't get it:

---

think

- As you read over the list of church leadership requirements, how do you stack up? Is this list too difficult to live up to? Why or why not?
- In what ways do you believe you live up to these requirements? Why?
- In order for people to follow your leadership, what are the areas in your life that need to change or improve?
- How can you begin to work on those areas starting today?
- What sorts of implications does this passage have for how you live in public and when no one is looking?
- How does integrity tie in to godly leadership?

pray

read Looking at Hearts, Not Faces

1 Samuel 16:4-13

Samuel did what GOD told him. When he arrived at Bethlehem, the town fathers greeted him, but apprehensively. "Is there something wrong?"

"Nothing's wrong. I've come to sacrifice this heifer and lead you in the worship of GOD. Prepare yourselves, be consecrated, and join me in worship." He made sure Jesse and his sons were also consecrated and called to worship.

When they arrived, Samuel took one look at Eliab and thought, "Here he is! GOD's anointed!"

But GOD told Samuel, "Looks aren't everything. Don't be impressed with his looks and stature. I've already eliminated him. GOD judges persons differently than humans do. Men and women look at the face; GOD looks into the heart."

Jesse then called up Abinadab and presented him to Samuel. Samuel said, "This man isn't GOD's choice either."

Next Jesse presented Shammah. Samuel said, "No, this man isn't either."

Jesse presented his seven sons to Samuel. Samuel was blunt with Jesse, "GOD hasn't chosen any of these."

Then he asked Jesse, "Is this it? Are there no more sons?"

"Well, yes, there's the runt. But he's out tending the sheep."

Samuel ordered Jesse, "Go get him. We're not moving from this spot until he's here."

Jesse sent for him. He was brought in, the very picture of health—bright-eyed, good-looking.

GOD said, "Up on your feet! Anoint him! This is the one."

Samuel took his flask of oil and anointed him, with his brothers standing around watching. The Spirit of GOD entered David like a rush of wind, God vitally empowering him for the rest of his life.

1 Timothy 4:12

And don't let anyone put you down because you're young. Teach believers with your life: by word, by demeanor, by love, by faith, by integrity.

---

first thoughts

like:

dislike:

agree:

disagree:

don't get it:

---

think

- As a young man, maybe you have heard someone tell you the same things David heard—that you were too young or that you didn't have enough experience, credentials, or accomplishments to make a difference yet. How do we refuse to let anyone look down upon us because of our age in a polite and respectful yet bold way?
- Even David's own father didn't think he had what it took to be a great leader, and yet the discouragement didn't prevent David from becoming a great and influential leader. What are some ways you can overcome other people's unbelief? Your own unbelief?
- Can you think of areas where people are looking down on your life because of your young age? What can be done about it specifically?
- What does it mean to not let anyone look down upon you because you are young? Is that active or passive? Aggressive or meek?

- Think about the five areas Paul encourages Timothy to model to others: word, demeanor, love, faith, and integrity. Of the five areas, which do you most need to improve in order to be a model to other believers?

pray

read Risky Business

From _The Next Generation Leader: Five Essentials for Those Who Will Shape the Future_ by Andy Stanley[1]

The leader who refuses to move until the fear is gone will never move. Consequently, he will never lead. There is always an uncertainty associated with the future. Uncertainty presupposes risk. Leadership is about moving boldly into the future in spite of uncertainty and risk. Without courage we will simply accumulate a collection of good ideas and regrets. What could be and should be will not be . . . at least not under our watch. Eventually somebody else will come along and seize the opportunity we passed up.

Ask veteran leaders about their risk-tolerance and they will all tell you the same thing: "I wish I had taken more risks." In other words, they wish they had not allowed their fear of the unknown to bridle their aspirations. Max De Pree made this observation: "An unwillingness to accept risk has swamped more leaders than anything I can think of."

Seasoned leaders rarely regret having taken risks. Even the risks that didn't pay off directly are viewed as a necessary part of the journey. A leader's regrets generally revolve around missed opportunities, not risks taken. Many of those missed opportunities would not have been missed had they been willing to push through their fear and embrace what could be. Fear, not a lack of good ideas, is usually what keeps a man or woman standing on the sidelines.

Fear of failure is common to man. But leaders view failure differently. Consequently, they don't fear failure in the same way the average individual does.

first thoughts

like:

dislike:

agree:

disagree:

don't get it:

Here's the difference: Eventually a leader's lust for progress overwhelms his reluctance to take risks. . . . Leaders know that the best way to ensure success is to take chances. While the average man or woman fears stepping out into a new opportunity, the leader fears missing out on a new opportunity. Being overly cautious leads to failure because caution can lead to missed opportunities. . . .

You can't lead without taking risk. You won't take risk without courage. Courage is essential to leadership.

think

- What connection exists between courage and leadership? In your opinion, is it possible to lead effectively without courage?
- What are your deepest fears? How do those fears keep you from stepping out and taking action?
- In what specific areas of your life is it worth it to you to take risks, even if you fail? Why?
- What do you regret when it comes to missed opportunities? What decisions would you have to make in order to eliminate any feelings of regret you may have in the future?
- How can other men challenge you to step up and take more risks? How can you help others do the same? Be specific.

pray

read The Courage to Lead

**From "The Leader of the Future: Harvard's Ronald Heifetz Offers a
Short Course on the Future of Leadership" by William C. Taylor**[2]

The real heroism of leadership involves having the courage to face reality — and
helping the people around you to face reality. It's no accident that the word
"vision" refers to our capacity to see. Of course, in business, vision has come
to mean something abstract or even inspirational. But the quality of any vision
depends on its accuracy, not just on its appeal or on how imaginative it is.

Mustering the courage to interrogate reality is a central function of a
leader. And that requires the courage to face three realities at once. First, what
values do we stand for — and are there gaps between those values and how we
actually behave? Second, what are the skills and talents of our company — and
are there gaps between those resources and what the market demands? Third,
what opportunities does the future hold — and are there gaps between those
opportunities and our ability to capitalize on them?

Now, don't get the wrong idea. Leaders don't answer those questions
themselves. That's the old definition of leadership: The leader has the

---

first thoughts

like:

dislike:

agree:

disagree:

don't get it:

---

answers — the vision — and everything else is a sales job to persuade people to sign up for it. Leaders certainly provide direction. But that often means posing well-structured questions, rather than offering definitive answers.

think

- This article is for business leaders, but how might it help influence the average man, no matter his occupation, to live his life?
- Why does being a leader involve so much courage?
- How can you be a leader in the midst of uncertainty? How does that relate to your everyday life?
- How does this leadership approach enter into the life of a follower of Christ?

pray

read A Leader's Motivation

Matthew 1:18-24; 2:12-15,19-21

The birth of Jesus took place like this. His mother, Mary, was engaged to be married to Joseph. Before they came to the marriage bed, Joseph discovered she was pregnant. (It was by the Holy Spirit, but he didn't know that.) Joseph, chagrined but noble, determined to take care of things quietly so Mary would not be disgraced.

While he was trying to figure a way out, he had a dream. God's angel spoke in the dream: "Joseph, son of David, don't hesitate to get married. Mary's pregnancy is Spirit-conceived. God's Holy Spirit has made her pregnant. She will bring a son to birth, and when she does, you, Joseph, will name him Jesus—'God saves'—because he will save his people from their sins." This would bring the prophet's embryonic sermon to full term:

Watch for this—a virgin will get pregnant and bear a son;
They will name him Immanuel (Hebrew for "God is with us").

Then Joseph woke up. He did exactly what God's angel commanded in the dream: He married Mary. But he did not consummate the marriage until she had the baby. He named the baby Jesus. . . .

In a dream, they were warned not to report back to Herod. So they worked out another route, left the territory without being seen, and returned to their own country.

After the scholars were gone, God's angel showed up again in Joseph's dream and commanded, "Get up. Take the child and his mother and flee to Egypt. Stay until further notice. Herod is on the hunt for this child, and wants to kill him."

Joseph obeyed. He got up, took the child and his mother under cover of darkness. They were out of town and well on their way by daylight. They lived in Egypt until Herod's death. This Egyptian exile fulfilled what Hosea had preached: "I called my son out of Egypt." . . .

Later, when Herod died, God's angel appeared in a dream to Joseph in Egypt: "Up, take the child and his mother and return to Israel. All those out to murder the child are dead."

Joseph obeyed. He got up, took the child and his mother, and reentered Israel.

---

first thoughts

like:

dislike:

agree:

disagree:

don't get it:

---

think

- When we read the story of Jesus' birth, we often focus on Jesus and Mary, but we skim over Joseph. Reread these verses and pay attention to Joseph's role.
- How does Joseph's obedience give you a better understanding of leadership? Who or what do you choose to be obedient to in your decision making?
- Joseph's obedient leadership always involved action and response. What are some ways you need to act in order to be a better leader?

- Joseph always put Mary's and Jesus' best interests above his own. Why did this make him a good leader?
- What are your motives in leadership?

pray

live   The Redefining

Take a few moments to skim through the notes you've made in these readings this week. What do they tell you about godly leadership as a man? Based on what you've read and discussed, is there anything that you want to change? Describe this below.

What, if anything, is stopping you from making this change?

How has your idea of leadership changed over the past week of this study?

How might growing in your leadership as a godly man affect your relationships, friendships, home life, work life, or school life for the better?

Talk with a close friend about all of the above. Brainstorm together about what it might take to move toward God in this area of your life. Determine what this looks like in a practical sense and then list any measurable goals you want to shoot for here. Review these goals each week to see how you are doing.

sharing
the load

Friends come and friends go,
    but a true friend sticks by you like family.

Proverbs 18:24

You use steel to sharpen steel,
    and one friend sharpens another.

Proverbs 27:17

a reminder

Before you dive into this study, spend a little time reviewing what you wrote in the previous lessons' Live sections. How are you doing? Check with your small-group members and review your progress toward the specified goals. If necessary, adjust your goals and plans and then recommit to them.

the defining line

When we think of women chatting at scrapbooking parties or talking on the phone for hours on end, we often roll our eyes. We're just not wired to share our feelings with other men the way women do with other women. But that shouldn't mean we don't share anything with each other at all. So what do healthy male relationships look like, relationships that challenge, sharpen, and encourage us to live up to our God-given potential?

John Donne said that no man is an island. But it seems that so many men try to live life that way—all by themselves. Developing healthy friendships with other men in which we do more than just talk about sports scores or play video games is essential to living as a godly man. We need others to help us on our spiritual journey with Christ as we are shaped and formed like Him more and more every day.

Describe what a healthy male friendship looks like to you.

How do you want your friends to challenge, sharpen, and encourage you? How do you want to do that for other men in your life?

Consider sharing your responses with your group when you meet.

read The Mightiest of Men

2 Samuel 23:8-23

This is the listing of David's top men.

Josheb-Basshebeth, the Tahkemonite. He was chief of the Three. He once put his spear to work against eight hundred—killed them all in a day.

Eleazar son of Dodai the Ahohite was the next of the elite Three. He was with David when the Philistines poked fun at them at Pas Dammim. When the Philistines drew up for battle, Israel retreated. But Eleazar stood his ground and killed Philistines right and left until he was exhausted—but he never let go of his sword! A big win for GOD that day. The army then rejoined Eleazar, but all there was left to do was the cleanup.

Shammah son of Agee the Hararite was the third of the Three. The Philistines had mustered for battle at Lehi, where there was a field full of lentils. Israel fled before the Philistines, but Shammah took his stand at the center of the field, successfully defended it, and routed the Philistines. Another great victory for GOD!

One day during harvest, the Three parted from the Thirty and joined David at the Cave of Adullam. A squad of Philistines had set up camp in the Valley of Rephaim. While David was holed up in the Cave, the Philistines had their base camp in Bethlehem. David had a sudden craving and said, "Would I ever like a drink of water from the well at the gate of Bethlehem!" So the Three penetrated the Philistine lines, drew water from the well at the gate of Bethlehem, and brought it back to David. But David wouldn't drink it; he poured it out as an offering to GOD, saying, "There is no way, GOD, that I'll drink this! This isn't mere water, it's their life-blood—they risked their very lives to bring it!" So David refused to drink it.

This is the sort of thing that the Three did.

Abishai brother of Joab and son of Zeruiah was the head of the Thirty. He once got credit for killing three hundred with his spear, but he was never named in the same breath as the Three. He was the most respected of the Thirty and was their captain, but never got included among the Three.

Benaiah son of Jehoiada from Kabzeel was a vigorous man who accomplished a great deal. He once killed two lion cubs in Moab. Another time, on a snowy day, he climbed down into a pit and killed a lion. Another time he killed a formidable Egyptian. The Egyptian was armed with a spear and Benaiah went against him with nothing but a walking stick; he seized the spear from his grip and killed him with his own spear.

These are the things that Benaiah son of Jehoiada is famous for. But neither did he ever get ranked with the Three. He was held in greatest respect among the Thirty, but he never got included with the Three. David put him in charge of his bodyguard.

---

first thoughts

like:

dislike:

agree:

disagree:

don't get it:

---

think

- David had thirty mighty men who were willing to die for him. Most people probably wouldn't have thirty, but do you have a few men around you who you consider mighty?
- Why did David feel it necessary to pour out the water the men had retrieved at the risk of their own lives?
- Are there times when you have had guys "retrieve water" for you? Why were they willing to do that for you?

- When have you "retrieved water" for other guys? Why did you do it? Was it worth it?
- What are a few ways you can "retrieve water" for your friends? Be specific.
- Do you think it is realistic in this day and age to have a list of your own "mighty men"? If so, how might you go about choosing them?

pray

read The Gift of Male Friendships

From *Life Together* by Dietrich Bonhoeffer[1]

But if there is so much blessing and joy even in a single encounter of brother with brother, how inexhaustible are the riches that open up for those who by God's will are privileged to live in the daily fellowship of life with other Christians! . . . It is easily forgotten that the fellowship of Christian brethren is a gift of grace, a gift of the Kingdom of God that any day may be taken from us, that the time that still separates us from utter loneliness may be brief indeed. Therefore, let him who until now has had the privilege of living a common Christian life with other Christians praise God's grace from the bottom of his heart. Let him thank God on his knees and declare: It is grace, nothing but grace, that we are allowed to live in community with Christian brethren.

---

first thoughts

like:

dislike:

agree:

disagree:

don't get it:

---

think

- When was the last time you felt "utter loneliness" in your life? Describe the situation.
- Why is it through God's grace that we are able to connect with other Christian guys?
- How can we grasp just how precious our friends really are?
- Who are your closest friends? When was the last time you thanked God—and them—for those friendships?

pray

read Holding Up the Hands of Others

Exodus 17:8-13

Amalek came and fought Israel at Rephidim. Moses ordered Joshua: "Select some men for us and go out and fight Amalek. Tomorrow I will take my stand on top of the hill holding God's staff."

Joshua did what Moses ordered in order to fight Amalek. And Moses, Aaron, and Hur went to the top of the hill. It turned out that whenever Moses raised his hands, Israel was winning, but whenever he lowered his hands, Amalek was winning. But Moses' hands got tired. So they got a stone and set it under him. He sat on it and Aaron and Hur held up his hands, one on each side. So his hands remained steady until the sun went down. Joshua defeated Amalek and its army in battle.

---

first thoughts

like:

dislike:

agree:

disagree:

don't get it:

---

think

- While Joshua was leading the Israelites in battle, Aaron and Hur held up Moses' hands. Do you think that Joshua, Aaron, and Hur understood the significance of their roles during the battle?
- When Moses' hands were raised, the Israelites were winning the battle; when his hands were lowered, they began to lose. Why do you think God orchestrated the battle to operate that way? What was God trying to communicate to the nation of Israel about His involvement?
- What can you learn from Aaron and Hur? How might their example be helpful in your interactions with your friends?
- Can you identify people in your life who need someone to hold up their hands for them, figuratively speaking?
- Who are your Aaron and Hur who hold you up when you get tired? Who can you be an Aaron or Hur for?

pray

read Sinners Anonymous

From "Worthy Relationships"[2]

Something that has been heavy on my heart lately is the struggle to develop relationships, to keep relationships and to heal broken relationships. Maybe the battle of the ages in the Church has always been our relationships with one another. Perhaps it is because that is what the world longs for most or maybe it is because the enemy is so jealous of our relationship with Jesus and with each other. The trust of knowing someone intimately is something he will never taste again so he strives to divide us.

The cry of our generation is for real, loving, caring, worth-dying-for relationships. When a group of young leaders were recently asked whether they would rather lead independently or as a team, overwhelmingly 95 percent said they would rather work together in a team leadership. Why is that? For me it isn't about having a position or being recognized, but it is about the relationships with others in the team and the process of wrestling together with God to see His purposes revealed. It is about putting together a puzzle where everyone has a piece to add making a mosaic of beauty that only God could produce. By myself I could never see produced what I see happen through a team of like-minded leaders. The excitement of pursuing a direction together, the joy of seeing God's hand move because of a unity and common purpose is the most fulfilling thing I can do. God loves relationships; Jesus would never have done what He did without His friends. He lived and died because of them and He rested the destiny of the human race on those same relationships. God the

first thoughts

like:

dislike:

agree:

disagree:

don't get it:

father gave Jesus friends. Don't you think He finds value in them? In the same breath, the enemy seeks to destroy the very relationships God seeks to produce. He uses our own sins to break them down. Pride of position, jealousy, envy, strife, those things that we call "our rights" all keep us from getting close to each other. Sometimes even Jesus and the word of God are used to justify breaking relationship or to shield us from others. Maybe someone has a different view or doctrine on the Bible that doesn't line up with ours. Maybe they are from a different Christian background than ours. Don't you think the world and the enemy stands back and laughs at us. Jesus spoke against the Pharisees' accusation that He was of the devil saying, "How can a Kingdom divided against itself stand?"

Doesn't that describe us as the Church sometimes? In any relationship, there must be risk, the risk of putting your heart out there and being exposed. It is a risky business, this issue of relationship, and it is one that cannot be resolved out of a position or title. Relationships are God-given, but they take work. My most valuable and treasured possessions are my relationships. They are more valuable than gold and I wouldn't trade them for the world. The friendships God has given me are friendships that will last an eternity. I believe the relationships that we have to fight for here on earth are the ones that will be key in eternity. Anything of value takes work and often the closest relationships I have have taken a lot of work and humility to keep. What is it worth to you?

I recently saw the last installment of *The Lord of the Rings* trilogy, *The Return of the King*. In the story, Tolkien focused the destiny of the world on the fellowship of the ring. A group of people from different cultures, countries and even races gathered together for one purpose, to save middle earth from the one who would destroy all life. Doesn't this sound like the battle we are in? If you have seen the movie or read the book, you know that the good guys win. But how did they win? They accomplished the task because they trusted, trusted beyond a hope and laid down even their very lives to see the goal accomplished. But in the end, it wasn't because of the task, it was because of the friendship that they would sacrifice so much.

Jesus put the trust of the godhead in His friends, He rested the destiny of the entire world in those same friends and He contends daily for relationship with us whom He calls friends. How much do you think friendship and relationship with others was worth to Jesus? He rested the future of the Kingdom of God—your future—on these relationships and He still does it today. The Kingdom of God is advanced through relationship, one person at a time. Now I ask, of how much value are your friends to you?

think

- Why is the pull to be known, to belong, so strong among our generation? Is this a good thing or a bad thing or both?
- The author says, "My most valuable and treasured possessions are my relationships. They are more valuable than gold and I wouldn't trade them for the world." Can you make such a statement? Why or why not?
- How should our relationship with Christ alter or enhance our relationships with those around us?
- How does trust play into your relationships with other guys? How can that trust be deepened in the coming weeks and months?
- How much do you value your friends? Have you been able to communicate that to them? Why or why not?

pray

read The Bond of Friendship

1 Samuel 18:1-4

By the time David had finished reporting to Saul, Jonathan was deeply impressed with David—an immediate bond was forged between them. He became totally committed to David. From that point on he would be David's number-one advocate and friend.

Saul received David into his own household that day, no more to return to the home of his father.

Jonathan, out of his deep love for David, made a covenant with him. He formalized it with solemn gifts: his own royal robe and weapons—armor, sword, bow, and belt.

1 Samuel 23:16-18

Jonathan, Saul's son, visited David at Horesh and encouraged him in God. He said, "Don't despair. My father, Saul, can't lay a hand on you. You will be Israel's king and I'll be right at your side to help. And my father knows it." Then the two of them made a covenant before GOD. David stayed at Horesh and Jonathan went home.

2 Samuel 1:26

> O my dear brother Jonathan,
>   I'm crushed by your death.
> Your friendship was a
>   miracle-wonder,
>   love far exceeding anything
>   I've known—
>   or ever hope to know.

first thoughts

like:

dislike:

agree:

disagree:

don't get it:

think

- The text says that Jonathan became David's number one advocate and friend. Who would you say is your number one advocate?
- Have you ever experienced a friendship with another guy that was so strong it could be described as "love far exceeding anything I've known—or ever hope to know"? Discuss or write your thoughts.
- This passage says that Jonathan and David made several covenants with one another. Why was making a covenant with one another so important?
- Have you ever made a specific commitment or vow to another friend like the one David and Jonathan made with each other? Are there specific commitments that you could implement into your relationships with other guys? What are they?

pray

live   The Redefining

Take a few moments to skim through the notes you've made in these readings. What do they tell you about godly male friendships? Based on what you've read and discussed, is there anything that you want to change? Describe this below.

What, if anything, is stopping you from making this change?

Who might be someone you could approach about sharing a mutual, intentional friendship in which you challenge, support, and encourage each other?

In what areas might you benefit from having intentional male friendships?

Talk with a close friend about all of the above. Brainstorm together about what it might take to move toward God in this area of your life. Determine what this looks like in a practical sense and then list any measurable goals you want to shoot for here. Review these goals each week to see how you are doing.

the female
species

Reverently honor an older woman as you would your
mother, and the younger women as sisters.

1 Timothy 5:2

a reminder

*Before you dive into this study, spend a little time reviewing what
you wrote in the previous lessons' Live sections. How are you doing?
Check with your small-group members and review your progress
toward the specified goals. If necessary, adjust your goals and plans
and then recommit to them.*

the defining line

If we're truly honest, interaction with women (especially when we are single)
can be difficult. It can get us into sticky situations. And it doesn't take Dr. Phil
to tell us that men and women interact, think, feel, talk, and behave differently.
We break into a cold sweat when we hear the question, "Do you think I look
fat in this dress?" We can't understand why women wouldn't want to spend
the entire weekend watching football or why they need to own over two dozen
pairs of shoes. Okay, maybe I'm being a little overdramatic here, but you get
the point: Men and women are different.

How we treat (or don't treat) women will reveal a lot about us. We must
take this seriously—very seriously—because they are our sisters in Christ.

Sure, we should value all people, but as men we need to take up the challenge to bring value to and affirm the strengths and gifts we see in women.

So how are we to interact with women in a healthy, God-honoring manner, whether our relationships with them are romantic or not?

What could or should we be doing to purely affirm our sisters in Christ?

Consider sharing your responses with your group when you meet.

read A Woman's Perspective

From *Captivating: Unveiling the Mystery of a Woman's Soul* by John and Stasi Eldredge[1]

I know I am not alone in this nagging sense of failing to measure up, a feeling of not being good enough as a woman. Every woman I've ever met feels it—something deeper than just the sense of failing at what she does. An underlying, gut feeling of failing at who she is. I am not enough, and I am too much at the same time. Not pretty enough, not thin enough, not kind enough, not gracious enough, too strong, too opinionated, too messy. The result is Shame, the universal companion of women. It haunts us, nipping at our heels, feeding on our deepest fear that we will end up abandoned and alone.

After all, if we were better women—whatever that means—life wouldn't be so hard. Right? We wouldn't have so many struggles; there would be less sorrow in our hearts. Why is it so hard to create meaningful friendships and sustain them? Why do our days seem so unimportant, filled not with romance and adventure but with duties and demands? We feel unseen, even by those who are closest to us. We feel unsought—that no one has the passion or the courage to pursue us, to get past our messiness to find the woman deep inside. And we feel uncertain—uncertain what it even means to be a woman; uncertain what it truly means to be feminine; uncertain if we are or ever will be.

---

first thoughts

like:

dislike:

agree:

disagree:

don't get it:

---

think

- It may seem a little strange to include an excerpt from a women's book in a discussion guide for guys. But as we all know, it's pretty valuable to try to understand women (although sometimes it may seem futile). From this particular excerpt, what can we learn?
- Based on Stasi Eldredge's words, how are the longings of men and women similar? How are they different?
- Do you know any women that feel a similar inadequacy?
- According to the author, most women feel unseen, unsought, and uncertain. What can we do to help the women we know feel seen, sought, and certain?

pray

read Friends or Not?

From _When Harry Met Sally_[2]

Harry Burns: You realize of course that we could never be friends.

Sally Albright: Why not?

Harry Burns: What I'm saying is—and this is not a come-on in any way, shape or form—is that men and women can't be friends because the sex part always gets in the way.

Sally Albright: That's not true. I have a number of men friends and there is no sex involved.

Harry Burns: No you don't.

Sally Albright: Yes I do.

Harry Burns: No you don't.

Sally Albright: Yes I do.

Harry Burns: You only think you do.

Sally Albright: You say I'm having sex with these men without my knowledge?

Harry Burns: No, what I'm saying is they all want to have sex with you.

Sally Albright: They do not.

Harry Burns: Do too.

Sally Albright: They do not.

Harry Burns: Do too.

Sally Albright: How do you know?

Harry Burns: Because no man can be friends with a woman that he finds attractive. He always wants to have sex with her.

Sally Albright: So, you're saying that a man can be friends with a woman he finds unattractive?

Harry Burns: No. You pretty much want to nail 'em too.

Sally Albright: What if they don't want to have sex with you?

Harry Burns: Doesn't matter because the sex thing is already out there so the friendship is ultimately doomed and that is the end of the story.

Sally Albright: Well, I guess we're not going to be friends then.

Harry Burns: I guess not.

Sally Albright: That's too bad.

---

first thoughts

like:

dislike:

agree:

disagree:

don't get it:

---

think

- In your opinion, is it possible for men and women to be just friends? Why or why not?
- Harry says that men and women can't be friends because "the sex part always gets in the way." Is it possible to be attracted to women and simultaneously remain pure? If so, how? If not, what influence, if any, does that have on our decision making?
- How do we find the balance in valuing a woman's physical beauty yet not seeing her as a sexual object?

pray

read The Perfect Wife?

Proverbs 31:10-31

A good woman is hard to find,
  and worth far more than diamonds.
Her husband trusts her without reserve,
  and never has reason to regret it.
Never spiteful, she treats him generously
  all her life long.
She shops around for the best yarns and cottons,
  and enjoys knitting and sewing.
She's like a trading ship that sails to faraway places
  and brings back exotic surprises.
She's up before dawn, preparing breakfast
  for her family and organizing her day.
She looks over a field and buys it,
  then, with money she's put aside, plants a garden.
First thing in the morning, she dresses for work,
  rolls up her sleeves, eager to get started.
She senses the worth of her work,
  is in no hurry to call it quits for the day.
She's skilled in the crafts of home and hearth,
  diligent in homemaking.
She's quick to assist anyone in need,
  reaches out to help the poor.
She doesn't worry about her family when it snows;
  their winter clothes are all mended and ready to wear.
She makes her own clothing,
  and dresses in colorful linens and silks.
Her husband is greatly respected
  when he deliberates with the city fathers.
She designs gowns and sells them,
  brings the sweaters she knits to the dress shops.
Her clothes are well-made and elegant,

and she always faces tomorrow with a smile.
When she speaks she has something worthwhile to say,
    and she always says it kindly.
She keeps an eye on everyone in her household,
    and keeps them all busy and productive.
Her children respect and bless her;
    her husband joins in with words of praise:
"Many women have done wonderful things,
    but you've outclassed them all!"
Charm can mislead and beauty soon fades.
    The woman to be admired and praised
    is the woman who lives in the Fear-of-God.
Give her everything she deserves!
    Festoon her life with praises!

Note to the single guy: We know there is a possibility that you may not even be close to marriage; therefore, this passage may or may not relate to you as much as other chapters. But we believe that there is something for all of us to learn in this passage, no matter what our marital status may be, so we recommend you complete this section as well as the others.

---

first thoughts

like:

dislike:

agree:

disagree:

don't get it:

---

think

- Do you think it's possible for a woman to live up to this standard? Why or why not?
- How does this passage compare to your own standards for a wife? In what ways are the similarities and differences positive or negative?
- How do these characteristics differ from what our culture values in women? How are they similar?
- This chapter is often referenced in Christian circles as the ideal for women, but what other insights or thoughts have you gleaned from reading this passage?
- If this is the "standard" we are to seek in a godly woman, by what standard should we be judged as guys?

pray

read Valuing Women (Part One)

John 4:1-30

Jesus realized that the Pharisees were keeping count of the baptisms that he and John performed (although his disciples, not Jesus, did the actual baptizing). They had posted the score that Jesus was ahead, turning him and John into rivals in the eyes of the people. So Jesus left the Judean countryside and went back to Galilee.

To get there, he had to pass through Samaria. He came into Sychar, a Samaritan village that bordered the field Jacob had given his son Joseph. Jacob's well was still there. Jesus, worn out by the trip, sat down at the well. It was noon.

A woman, a Samaritan, came to draw water. Jesus said, "Would you give me a drink of water?" (His disciples had gone to the village to buy food for lunch.)

The Samaritan woman, taken aback, asked, "How come you, a Jew, are asking me, a Samaritan woman, for a drink?" (Jews in those days wouldn't be caught dead talking to Samaritans.)

Jesus answered, "If you knew the generosity of God and who I am, you would be asking me for a drink, and I would give you fresh, living water."

The woman said, "Sir, you don't even have a bucket to draw with, and this well is deep. So how are you going to get this 'living water'? Are you a better man than our ancestor Jacob, who dug this well and drank from it, he and his sons and livestock, and passed it down to us?"

Jesus said, "Everyone who drinks this water will get thirsty

first thoughts

like:

dislike:

agree:

disagree:

don't get it:

again and again. Anyone who drinks the water I give will never thirst—not ever. The water I give will be an artesian spring within, gushing fountains of endless life."

The woman said, "Sir, give me this water so I won't ever get thirsty, won't ever have to come back to this well again!"

He said, "Go call your husband and then come back."

"I have no husband," she said.

"That's nicely put: 'I have no husband.' You've had five husbands, and the man you're living with now isn't even your husband. You spoke the truth there, sure enough."

"Oh, so you're a prophet! Well, tell me this: Our ancestors worshiped God at this mountain, but you Jews insist that Jerusalem is the only place for worship, right?"

"Believe me, woman, the time is coming when you Samaritans will worship the Father neither here at this mountain nor there in Jerusalem. You worship guessing in the dark; we Jews worship in the clear light of day. God's way of salvation is made available through the Jews. But the time is coming—it has, in fact, come—when what you're called will not matter and where you go to worship will not matter.

"It's who you are and the way you live that count before God. Your worship must engage your spirit in the pursuit of truth. That's the kind of people the Father is out looking for: those who are simply and honestly *themselves* before him in their worship. God is sheer being itself—Spirit. Those who worship him must do it out of their very being, their spirits, their true selves, in adoration."

The woman said, "I don't know about that. I do know that the Messiah is coming. When he arrives, we'll get the whole story."

"I am he," said Jesus. "You don't have to wait any longer or look any further."

Just then his disciples came back. They were shocked. They couldn't believe he was talking with that kind of a woman. No one said what they were all thinking, but their faces showed it.

The woman took the hint and left. In her confusion she left her water pot. Back in the village she told the people, "Come see a man who knew all about the things I did, who knows me inside and out. Do you think this could be the Messiah?" And they went out to see for themselves.

think

- We know that Jesus was God, but we often underplay His humanity. Notice in this passage how Jesus the man valued this woman, especially a Samaritan woman (Samaritans were despised by the Jews). What specifically did Jesus do to show her value?
- How can you specifically value women as Jesus does?
- What's the balance between valuing women and being overly flirtatious or misleading?

pray

read Valuing Women (Part Two)

Ruth 2

It so happened that Naomi had a relative by marriage, a man prominent and rich, connected with Elimelech's family. His name was Boaz.

One day Ruth, the Moabite foreigner, said to Naomi, "I'm going to work; I'm going out to glean among the sheaves, following after some harvester who will treat me kindly."

Naomi said, "Go ahead, dear daughter."

And so she set out. She went and started gleaning in a field, following in the wake of the harvesters. Eventually she ended up in the part of the field owned by Boaz, her father-in-law Elimelech's relative. A little later Boaz came out from Bethlehem, greeting his harvesters, "GOD be with you!" They replied, "And GOD bless you!"

Boaz asked his young servant who was foreman over the farm hands, "Who is this young woman? Where did she come from?"

The foreman said, "Why, that's the Moabite girl, the one who came with Naomi from the country of Moab. She asked permission. 'Let me glean,' she said, 'and gather among the sheaves following after your harvesters.' She's been at it steady ever since, from early morning until now, without so much as a break."

Then Boaz spoke to Ruth: "Listen, my daughter. From now on don't go to any other field to glean—stay right here in this one. And stay close to my young women. Watch where they are harvesting and follow them. And don't worry about a thing; I've given orders to my servants not to harass you. When you get thirsty, feel free to go and drink from the water buckets that the servants have filled."

She dropped to her knees, then bowed her face to the ground. "How does this happen that you should pick me out and treat me so kindly—*me*, a foreigner?"

Boaz answered her, "I've heard all about you—heard about the way you treated your mother-in-law after the death of her husband, and how you left your father and mother and the land of your birth and have come to live among a bunch of total strangers. GOD reward you well for what you've done—and with a generous bonus besides from GOD, to whom you've come seeking protection under his wings."

She said, "Oh sir, such grace, such kindness—I don't deserve it. You've touched my heart, treated me like one of your own. And I don't even belong here!"

At the lunch break, Boaz said to her, "Come over here; eat some bread. Dip it in the wine."

So she joined the harvesters. Boaz passed the roasted grain to her. She ate her fill and even had some left over.

When she got up to go back to work, Boaz ordered his servants: "Let her glean where there's still plenty of grain on the ground—make it easy for her. Better yet, pull some of the good stuff out and leave it for her to glean. Give her special treatment."

Ruth gleaned in the field until evening. When she threshed out what she had gathered, she ended up with nearly a full sack of barley! She gathered up her gleanings, went back to town, and showed her mother-in-law the results of her day's work; she also gave her the leftovers from her lunch.

Naomi asked her, "So where did you glean today? Whose field? GOD bless whoever it was who took such good care of you!"

Ruth told her mother-in-law, "The man with whom I worked today? His name is Boaz."

Naomi said to her daughter-in-law, "Why, GOD bless that man! GOD hasn't quite walked out on us after all! He still loves us, in bad times as well as good!"

Naomi went on, "That man, Ruth, is one of our circle of covenant redeemers, a close relative of ours!"

Ruth the Moabitess said, "Well, listen to this: He also told me, 'Stick with my workers until my harvesting is finished.'"

Naomi said to Ruth, "That's wonderful, dear daughter! Do that! You'll be safe in the company of his young women; no danger now of being raped in some stranger's field."

So Ruth did it—she stuck close to Boaz's young women, gleaning in the fields daily until both the barley and wheat harvesting were finished. And she continued living with her mother-in-law.

---

first thoughts

like:

dislike:

agree:

disagree:

don't get it:

---

think

- How did Boaz value Ruth in this passage?
- What can we as guys learn from Boaz and his interaction with Ruth? What are some practical elements of his interaction that we can emulate?
- What are some ways you consciously or subconsciously evaluate and assess women's value? Is it healthy or unhealthy? Why or why not?
- Admit it: It can be easy to value women who are attractive, socially adept, and seem to have it all together. But what can we

do to value women who are less than easy on the eyes or less than socially acceptable or just simply on the fringe, as Ruth was?

pray

live   The Redefining

Take a few moments to skim through the notes you've made in these readings. What do they tell you about relationships with women? Based on what you've read and discussed, is there anything that you want to change? Describe this below.

What, if anything, is stopping you from making this change?

If you were to sit down with three of your closest female friends and ask them to what extent you affirm and value them as women, what might they say?

Why is interacting with women awkward at times? What could be done to make the awkwardness dissipate? (Or is that impossible?)

Talk with a close friend about all of the above. Brainstorm together about what it might take to move toward God in this area of your life. Determine what this looks like in a practical sense and then list any measurable goals you want to shoot for here. Review these goals each week to see how you are doing.

the life of
integrity

And don't let anyone put you down because you're
young. Teach believers with your life: by word, by
demeanor, by love, by faith, by integrity.

1 Timothy 4:12

GOD can't stand deceivers,
    but oh how he relishes integrity.

Proverbs 11:20

a reminder

*Before you dive into this study, spend a little time reviewing what
you wrote in the previous lessons' Live sections. How are you doing?
Check with your small-group members and review your progress
toward the specified goals. If necessary, adjust your goals and plans
and then recommit to them.*

the defining line

We see a lot of hypocrisy in our world. Many people live one way in the
public eye and another way behind closed doors. We see this especially with
politicians, businessmen, and, sadly, even Christian leaders. Many times, people
far from God see this two-faced behavior of Christ-followers. As a result, it

turns them off to a relationship with God. It was Gandhi who said that if it weren't for the behavior of Christians, he would be a Christian. Integrity and consistency in our lives is extremely important in relationship to our witness as followers of Jesus.

In the broader sense of the word, how would you define integrity (i.e., more than just "being honest")?

Think about this past week. How have your words matched your actions?

Consider sharing your responses with your group when you meet.

read Holding Fast, Not Loosening My Grip

Job 2:1-10

One day when the angels came to report to GOD, Satan also showed up. GOD singled out Satan, saying, "And what have you been up to?" Satan answered GOD, "Oh, going here and there, checking things out." Then GOD said to Satan, "Have you noticed my friend Job? There's no one quite like him, is there — honest and true to his word, totally devoted to God and hating evil? He still has a firm grip on his integrity! You tried to trick me into destroying him, but it didn't work."

Satan answered, "A human would do anything to save his life. But what do you think would happen if you reached down and took away his health? He'd curse you to your face, that's what."

GOD said, "All right. Go ahead — you can do what you like with him. But mind you, don't kill him."

Satan left GOD and struck Job with terrible sores. Job was ulcers and scabs from head to foot. They itched and oozed so badly that he took a piece of broken pottery to scrape himself, then went and sat on a trash heap, among the ashes.

His wife said, "Still holding on to your precious integrity, are you? Curse God and be done with it!"

He told her, "You're talking like an empty-headed fool. We take the good days from God — why not also the bad days?"

Not once through all this did Job sin. He said nothing against God.

Job 27:1-6

Having waited for Zophar, Job now resumed his defense:

"God-Alive! He's denied me justice!
    God Almighty! He's ruined my life!
But for as long as I draw breath,
    and for as long as God breathes life into me,

I refuse to say one word that isn't true.
　　I refuse to confess to any charge that's false.
There is no way I'll ever agree to your accusations.
　　I'll not deny my integrity even if it costs me my life.
I'm holding fast to my integrity and not loosening my grip—
　　and, believe me, I'll never regret it.

---

first thoughts

like:

dislike:

agree:

disagree:

don't get it:

---

think

- Why do you think Job's integrity was so important to him that he wouldn't deny God and what was right, even if his decision cost him his life? Is maintaining your integrity that important to you? Why or why not?
- Have you ever felt like Job, tempted to sell out and curse God in the midst of sorrow or another circumstance? Why or why not?
- How might we learn from Job, who clung to his integrity while his wife encouraged him to curse God?

pray

read The Integrity Dilemma

From "Becoming People of Integrity" by Stephen L. Carter[1]

My first lesson in integrity came the hard way. It was 1960 or thereabouts and I was a first-grader at P.S. 129 in Harlem. The teacher had us all sitting in a circle, playing a game in which each child would take a turn donning a blindfold and then trying to identify objects by touch alone as she handed them to us. If you guessed right, you stayed in until the next round. If you guessed wrong, you were out. I survived almost to the end, amazing the entire class with my abilities. Then, to my dismay, the teacher realized what I had known and relied upon from the start: my blindfold was tied imperfectly and a sliver of bright reality leaked in from outside. By holding the unknown object in my lap instead of out in front of me, as most of the other children did, I could see at least a corner or a side and sometimes more—but always enough to figure out what it was. So my remarkable success was due only to my ability to break the rules.

Fortunately for my own moral development, I was caught. And as a result of being caught, I suffered, in front of my classmates, a humiliating reminder of right and wrong: I had cheated at the game. Cheating was wrong. It was that simple.

---

first thoughts

like:

dislike:

agree:

disagree:

don't get it:

I do not remember many of the details of the public lecture that I received from my teacher. I do remember that I was made to feel terribly ashamed; and it is good that I was made to feel that way, for I had something to be ashamed of. The moral opprobrium that accompanied that shame was sufficiently intense that it has stayed with me ever since, which is exactly how shame is supposed to work. And as I grew older, whenever I was even tempted to cheat—at a game, on homework—I would remember my teacher's stern face and the humiliation of sitting before my classmates, revealed to the world as a cheater.

That was then, this is now. Browsing recently in my local bookstore, I came across a book that boldly proclaimed on its cover that it contained instructions on how to cheat—the very word occurred in the title—at a variety of video games. My instincts tell me that this cleverly chosen title is helping the book to sell very well. For it captures precisely what is wrong with America today: we care far more about winning than about playing by the rules.

Consider just a handful of examples, drawn from headlines of the mid-1990s: the winner of the Miss Virginia pageant is stripped of her title after officials determine that her educational credentials are false; a television network is forced to apologize for using explosives to add a bit of versimilitude to a tape purporting to show that a particular truck is unsafe; and the authors of a popular book on management are accused of using bulk purchases at key stores to manipulate the *New York Times* best-seller list. Go back a few more years and we can add in everything from a slew of Wall Street titans imprisoned for violating a bewildering variety of laws in their frantic effort to get ahead, to the women's Boston Marathon winner branded a cheater for spending part of the race on the subway. But cheating is evidently no big deal: some 70 percent of college students admit to having done it at least once.

That, in a nutshell, is America's integrity dilemma: we are all full of fine talk about how desperately our society needs it, but, when push comes to shove, we would just as soon be on the winning side. A couple of years ago as I sat watching a football game with my children, trying to explain to them what was going on, I was struck by an event I had often noticed but on which I had never reflected. A player who failed to catch a ball thrown his way hit the ground, rolled over, and then jumped up, celebrating as though he had caught the pass after all. The referee was standing in a position that did not give him a good view of what had happened, was fooled by the player's pretense, and so moved the ball down the field. The player rushed back to the huddle so that his team could run another play before the officials had a chance to review the tape. (Until 1993, National Football League officials could watch a television replay and change their call, as long as the next play had not been run.) But viewers at home did have the benefit of the replay, and we saw what the referee missed: the ball lying on the ground instead of snug in the receiver's hands. The only comment from the broadcasters: "What a heads-up play!" Meaning: "Wow, what a great liar this kid is! Well done!"

think

- Think back to a specific time when you learned firsthand a major lesson in integrity. What did you learn? What were you feeling? Why?
- The author lists several examples of those in the public eye who cheated. Can you think of examples in the media? How about specific examples of people you know?
- Why is it that our world values winning and success over integrity?
- How much do you experience the integrity dilemma in your own life?
- How tempting is it to be seen as successful rather than full of integrity?

pray

read Cross-Examined

Psalm 26

Clear my name, GOD;
> I've kept an honest shop.
I've thrown in my lot with you, GOD, and
> I'm not budging.

Examine me, GOD, from head to foot,
> order your battery of tests.
Make sure I'm fit
> inside and out

So I never lose
> sight of your love,
But keep in step with you,
> never missing a beat.

I don't hang out with tricksters,
> I don't pal around with thugs;
I hate that pack of gangsters,
> I don't deal with double-dealers.

I scrub my hands with purest soap,
> then join hands with the others in the great circle,
> dancing around your altar, GOD,
Singing God-songs at the top of my lungs,
> telling God-stories.

GOD, I love living with you;
> your house glows with your glory.
When it's time for spring cleaning,
> don't sweep me out with the quacks and crooks,

Men with bags of dirty tricks,
  women with purses stuffed with bribe-money.

You know I've been aboveboard with you;
  now be aboveboard with me.
I'm on the level with you, GOD;
  I bless you every chance I get.

---

first thoughts

like:

dislike:

agree:

disagree:

don't get it:

---

think

- What can David teach us about being completely honest and open before our Creator?
- If you were to write a psalm to God, could you write the words of this one and be telling the truth?
- Is it possible for us to live with integrity before others if we can't first live with honesty and an open heart before God?
- Is it possible for us to worship God with a dishonest heart or a spirit unwilling to be upright before Him? Why or why not?
- What can you learn from this psalm about how to order your private life? Be specific.

pray

read Compromising for Success

From "Mr. Dirty Comes Clean: In a Compelling Book, Former NFL Hit Man Bill Romanowski Reveals How He Became Football's Most Feared Player," an interview with Nate Penn[2]

You've said you would do almost anything to get a competitive edge. Where did you draw the line?

The line was always moving. Sometimes, it was about illegal or legal, and "Could I get away with it?" Sometimes, it was "Would this create a positive drug test?" but one thing I would never do is compromise maximum effort in getting ready for a game or getting ready for an upcoming season. Being my best every time I took the field was the most important thing to me.

What in your mind, looking back, is the very first time you crossed the line? The point after which everything was different?

Probably taking phentermine.

---

first thoughts

like:

dislike:

agree:

disagree:

don't get it:

Did you feel guilty about taking phentermine? What was running through your mind?

No. I was caught up in being the absolute best I could be, in getting ready for the next game, the next season, the next workout—I was so blinded by what I had to do to be the best I could be to compete that there's a part of me that didn't really analyze and look at what I was doing all the time.

think

- For Bill Romanowski, the most important thing was getting an advantage on the field, even if his methods were illegal. For you, the temptation may not be to take steroids to be the best athlete. But what are you tempted to fudge on in order to get ahead or look better in the eyes of others?
- Romanowski said, "The line was always moving." What is the line for you between truth and dishonesty? When are you most tempted to move the line? Be specific.
- When, if at all, are you are so blinded by your ambition that you are unable to make wise decisions? Is there anything you can do about that? How can other guys help you when you become blinded?

pray

read Integrated Integrity

Proverbs 14:32

The evil of bad people leaves them out in the cold;
   the integrity of good people creates a safe place for living.

Proverbs 16:11

GOD cares about honesty in the workplace;
   your business is his business.

Proverbs 20:28

Love and truth form a good leader;
   sound leadership is founded on loving integrity.

---

first thoughts

like:

dislike:

agree:

disagree:

don't get it:

---

think

- How might the integrity of good people create a safe place for living? What might that look like in your life?
- Why do you think God cares so much about integrity?
- Can you ever honor God and simultaneously lack integrity?
- Proverbs is a guide for wise living. Why is it wise for us to be honest and upright in how we live our lives among other people? Be specific.

pray

live   The Redefining

Take a few moments to skim through the notes you've made in these readings. What do they tell you about being a man of integrity? Based on what you've read and discussed, is there anything that you want to change? Describe this below.

What, if anything, is stopping you from making this change?

What is the central area of your life—big or small—in which integrity needs to be more evident? Is it in your finances, your thought life, truth telling, your friendships, relationships at work, or something else? List the main area in the space below.

What are some specific ways that others in your small group can encourage you to be more honest in the way you live as a man who is following Christ? How can you help other guys in your small group in the same way?

Talk with a close friend about all of the above. Brainstorm together about what it might take to move toward God in this area of your life. Determine what this looks like in a practical sense and then list any measurable goals you want to shoot for here. Review these goals each week to see how you are doing.

picking up
the towel

"It's not going to be that way with you. Whoever wants to be great must become a servant. Whoever wants to be first among you must be your slave. That is what the Son of Man has done: He came to serve, not be served—and then to give away his life in exchange for the many who are held hostage."

Matthew 20:26-28

a reminder

Before you dive into this study, spend a little time reviewing what you wrote in the previous lessons' Live sections. How are you doing? Check with your small-group members and review your progress toward the specified goals. If necessary, adjust your goals and plans and then recommit to them.

the defining line

God's redemptive plan for the world didn't involve conquering governments or overthrowing oppressive kings or forcing everyone on earth to bow down to Him. His redemptive plan used the most ironic of all strategies: serving others. Instead of standing elevated on a platform of applause, He chose to kneel down and touch the untouchable, comfort the neglected, and hold the broken. We've heard it in church a million times: We're called to serve others.

But what does that really mean on a day-to-day basis? What does that look like on a Tuesday afternoon?

Make a list of the people you know who truly have genuine hearts that desire to serve.

In what ways does your upbringing influence your thoughts about serving others, good or bad?

Describe a time when you experienced a deep sense of joy from serving someone else.

Consider sharing your responses with your group when you meet.

read Attitude Check

Philippians 2:1-11

If you've gotten anything at all out of following Christ, if his love has made any difference in your life, if being in a community of the Spirit means anything to you, if you have a heart, if you *care*—then do me a favor: Agree with each other, love each other, be deep-spirited friends. Don't push your way to the front; don't sweet-talk your way to the top. Put yourself aside, and help others get ahead. Don't be obsessed with getting your own advantage. Forget yourselves long enough to lend a helping hand.

Think of yourselves the way Christ Jesus thought of himself. He had equal status with God but didn't think so much of himself that he had to cling to the advantages of that status no matter what. Not at all. When the time came, he set aside the privileges of deity and took on the status of a slave, became *human*! Having become human, he stayed human. It was an incredibly humbling process. He didn't claim special privileges. Instead, he lived a selfless, obedient life and then died a selfless, obedient death—and the worst kind of death at that—a crucifixion.

Because of that obedience, God lifted him high and honored him far beyond anyone or anything, ever, so that all created beings in heaven and on earth—even those long ago dead and buried—will bow in worship before this Jesus Christ, and call out in praise that he is the Master of all, to the glorious honor of God the Father.

first thoughts
like:
dislike:
agree:
disagree:
don't get it:

think

- Can you name one or two men you know who model this type of lifestyle to their friends, family, neighbors, and coworkers? What is it about them that makes them come to mind?
- Paul's words fly in the face of everything our culture communicates to us when it comes to how we are to act in the world. If someone lived out verses 2-4, how might the world view that individual?
- In what specific areas of your life were you challenged to imitate the life of Christ as you read this passage?
- What does it mean for you to take on the status of a slave, like Christ did? Be specific.

pray

read Others-Minded

Acts 2:42-46

They committed themselves to the teaching of the apostles, the life together, the common meal, and the prayers.

Everyone around was in awe—all those wonders and signs done through the apostles! And all the believers lived in a wonderful harmony, holding everything in common. They sold whatever they owned and pooled their resources so that each person's need was met.

They followed a daily discipline of worship in the Temple followed by meals at home, every meal a celebration, exuberant and joyful.

Acts 4:32-37

The whole congregation of believers was united as one—one heart, one mind! They didn't even claim ownership of their own possessions. No one said, "That's mine; you can't have it." They shared everything. The apostles gave powerful witness to the resurrection of the Master Jesus, and grace was on all of them.

And so it turned out that not a person among them was needy. Those who owned fields or houses sold them and brought the price of the sale to the apostles and made an offering of it. The apostles then distributed it according to each person's need.

Joseph, called by the apostles "Barnabas" (which means "Son of Comfort"), a Levite born in

first thoughts
like:
dislike:
agree:
disagree:
don't get it:

Cyprus, sold a field that he owned, brought the money, and made an offering of it to the apostles.

think

- Think about the passage you just read. Do you believe this level of sacrifice and willingness to serve is realistic in our culture today? Why or why not?
- Acts says that the believers "pooled their resources so that each person's need was met." How does this phrase relate to our responsibility and concern for the poor in our communities?
- To what extent can servanthood be connected to generosity of our time, resources, energies, and skills?
- Why is it so difficult for us to serve others?

pray

read Holy Ambition?

Philippians 2:3

Don't push your way to the front; don't sweet-talk your way to the top. Put yourself aside, and help others get ahead.

From "Ambition and Its Enemies: A Secret of America's Success, It Both Prods Us to Achievement and Condemns Us to Failure" by Robert J. Samuelson[1]

We are a nation of ambitious people, and yet ambition is a quality that is hard to praise and easy to deplore. It's a great engine of American creativity, but it also can be an unrelenting oppressor, which robs us of time and peace of mind. Especially in highly prosperous periods — periods like the present — it becomes fashionable to question whether ambition has gotten out of hand and is driving us to excesses of striving and craving that are self-destructive. . . .

One-upsmanship is a national mania. You see it every time a wide receiver prances into the end zone and raises his index finger in a triumphant "We're No. 1" salute, even if his team is mired in a losing season. More common is the search for status symbols — a bigger house, a more exotic vacation, a niftier bike, a faster computer — that separate us from the crowd. Money may not be the only way to satisfy this urge, but it's the most common because it can so easily translate itself into some other badge of identity and standing.

What people disdain as ambition they also venerate as opportunity. As Tocqueville long ago noted, America was built on the notion that — unlike Europe, with its hereditary aristocracy — people could write their own life stories. The ideal endures. A 1996 survey asked whether anyone starting poor could become rich; 78 percent of Americans thought so. But it's not just the economy or even politics. Social standing is fluid everywhere. Ambition and its creative powers permeate the arts, the professions, academia, science. Because everyone can be someone, the competition to rise above the crowd is unrelenting and often ruthless.

Few of us escape ambition's wounds. There are damaged dreams, abandoned projects and missed promotions. Most of us face the pressures of balancing competing demands between our inner selves and outer lives. A society that peddles so many extravagant promises sows much disappointment. Ambition is bitter as often as sweet; but without it, we'd be sunk.

---

first thoughts

like:

dislike:

agree:

disagree:

don't get it:

---

think

- Is it possible to be a driven, ambitious person and serve Christ and others at the same time? If not, why not? If so, how?
- Is it possible to reconcile the verse from Philippians 2:3 and the article excerpt?
- Why is ambition seen as so good in America? Is your ambition more American or biblical or somewhere in between? Why? How did it get there?

pray

read Dirty Feet

John 13:1-17

Just before the Passover Feast, Jesus knew that the time had come to leave this world to go to the Father. Having loved his dear companions, he continued to love them right to the end. It was suppertime. The Devil by now had Judas, son of Simon the Iscariot, firmly in his grip, all set for the betrayal.

Jesus knew that the Father had put him in complete charge of everything, that he came from God and was on his way back to God. So he got up from the supper table, set aside his robe, and put on an apron. Then he poured water into a basin and began to wash the feet of the disciples, drying them with his apron. When he got to Simon Peter, Peter said, "Master, *you* wash *my* feet?"

Jesus answered, "You don't understand now what I'm doing, but it will be clear enough to you later."

Peter persisted, "You're not going to wash my feet—ever!"

Jesus said, "If I don't wash you, you can't be part of what I'm doing."

"Master!" said Peter. "Not only my feet, then. Wash my hands! Wash my head!"

Jesus said, "If you've had a bath in the morning, you only need your feet washed now and you're clean from head to toe. My concern, you understand, is holiness, not hygiene. So now you're clean. But not every one of you." (He knew who was betraying him. That's why he said, "Not every one of you.") After he had finished washing their feet, he took his robe, put it back on, and went back to his place at the table.

Then he said, "Do you understand what I have done to you? You address me as 'Teacher' and 'Master,' and rightly so. That is what I am. So if I, the Master and Teacher, washed your feet, you must now wash each other's feet. I've laid down a pattern for you. What I've done, you do. I'm only pointing out the obvious. A servant is not ranked above his master; an employee doesn't give orders to the employer. If you understand what I'm telling you, act like it—and live a blessed life.

---

first thoughts

like:

dislike:

agree:

disagree:

don't get it:

---

think

- What might have been going through the minds of the disciples as Jesus prepared to do a job that only a slave would have performed in that culture?
- In verse 12 Jesus asked, "Do you understand what I have done to you?" Turn the tables for a moment: Do you understand the implications that this story has on us?
- Jesus also said in verse 15, "I've laid down a pattern for you. What I've done, you do." How are we to do this? What steps will have to occur for this to take place?

- How might other men begin to view you if you were known as being a servant of others in the classroom, the family room, or the boardroom?
- What sacrifices would it take on your part for you to live the towel-bearing lifestyle?

pray

read Servant Leadership

From *Quotes for the Journey, Wisdom for the Way* compiled by Gordon S. Jackson[2]

> You can tell whether you are becoming a servant by how you act when people treat you like one.
>
> Gordon MacDonald

> If you wish to be a leader you will be frustrated, for very few people wish to be led. If you aim to be a servant, you will never be frustrated.
>
> Frank F. Warren

---

first thoughts

like:

dislike:

agree:

disagree:

don't get it:

---

think

- Look at the first quote again. Think of a time when you were treated like a servant. How did you feel? How did you react? Why?
- Describe a time when you have treated other people like a servant, whether consciously or subconsciously.
- We hear the buzzwords *servant leadership* thrown around a lot these days. What does it mean to be a servant leader? Be specific and practical.
- What difference does service make? How does it play into your identity?

pray

live   The Redefining

Take a few moments to skim through the notes you've made in these readings. What do they tell you about God-honoring and Christ-modeled service? Based on what you've read and discussed, is there anything that you want to change? Describe this below.

What, if anything, is stopping you from making this change?

How will your mindset and your lifestyle need to change if you are to be recognized as a man of the towel?

How will this change of perspective influence your attitude or ability to lead and serve others close to you?

Who can help and challenge you to become more of a servant to others?

Talk with a close friend about all of the above. Brainstorm together about what it might take to move toward God in this area of your life. Determine what this looks like in a practical sense and then list any measurable goals you want to shoot for here. Review these goals each week to see how you are doing.

Even though you've reached the end of this discussion guide, moving toward a better understanding of what it means to be a godly man should continue. Let what has begun during this time continue to redefine what it means for you to be a committed, devoted, passionate, and loyal man of God. Continue to process with other men what it means to love and serve and lead as Jesus Himself did when He walked this earth as a man. Commit to discussing your goals and discoveries with small-group members or other close guy friends. And, after some time has passed, review this book. Refresh yourself on the areas in which you have been challenged and stretched. Finally, ask God to help you be the man He desires you to be.

discussion group
study tips

After going through the study on your own, it's time to sit down with others and go deeper. A group of eight to ten is optimal, but smaller groups will allow members to participate more.

Here are a few thoughts on how to make the most of your group discussion time.

Set ground rules. You don't need many. Here are two:

First, you'll want group members to make a commitment to the entire eight-week study. A binding legal document with notarized signatures and commitments written in blood probably isn't necessary—but *you* know your friends best. Just remember this: Significant personal growth happens when group members spend enough time together to really get to know each other. Hit-and-miss attendance rarely allows this to occur.

Second, agree together that everyone's story is important. Time is a valuable commodity, so if you have only an hour to spend together, do your best to give each person ample time to express concerns, pass along insights, and generally feel like a participating member of the group. Small-group discussions are not monologues.

Meet regularly. Choose a time and place and stick to it. No one likes showing up to a restaurant at noon, only to discover that the meeting was moved to seven in the evening at so-and-so's house. Consistency removes stress that could otherwise frustrate discussion and subsequent personal growth. It's only eight weeks. You can do this.

Think ahead. Whoever is leading or organizing the study needs to keep an eye on the calendar. No matter what day or time you pick, you're probably going to run into a date that just doesn't work for people. Maybe it's a holiday. Maybe there's a huge concert or conference in town. Maybe there's a random week when everyone is going to be out of town. Keep in communication with each other about the meetings and be flexible if you do have to reschedule a meeting or skip a week.

Talk openly. If you enter this study with shields up, you're probably not alone. And you're not a "bad person" for your hesitation to unpack your life in front of friends or strangers. Maybe you're skeptical about the value of revealing the deepest parts of who you are to others. Maybe you're simply too afraid of what might fall out of the suitcase. You don't have to go to a place where you're uncomfortable. If you want to sit and listen, offer a few thoughts, or even express a surface level of your own pain, go ahead. But don't neglect what brings you to this place—that desperation. You can't ignore it away. Dip your feet in the water of brutally honest discussion and you may choose to dive in. There is healing here.

Stay on task. Be wary of sharing material that falls into the Too Much Information (TMI) category. Don't spill unnecessary stuff. This is about discovering how *you* can be a better person.

Hold each other accountable. The Live section is an important gear in the "redefinition" machine. If you're really ready for positive change—for spiritual growth—you'll want to take this section seriously. Get personal when you summarize your discoveries. Be practical as you compose your goals. And make sure you're realistic as you determine a plan for accountability. Be extraordinarily loving but brutally honest as you examine each other's Live sections. The stuff on this page must be doable. Don't hold back—this is where the rubber meets the road.

frequently asked
questions

I'm stuck. I've read the words on the page, but they just don't connect. Am I missing something?

Be patient. There's no need for speed-reading. Reread the words. Pray about them. Reflect on the questions at the bottom of the page. Consider rewriting the reading in a way that makes sense to you. Meditate on one idea at a time. Read Scripture passages in different Bible translations. Ask a friend for help. Skip the section and come back to it later. And don't beat yourself up if you still don't connect. Turn the page and keep seeking.

This study includes a wide variety of readings. Some are intended to provoke. Others are intended to subdue. Some are meant to apply to a thinker, others to a feeler, and still others to an experiential learner. If your groove is pop culture, science, relationships, art, or something completely different, there's something in here that you're naturally going to click with, but that doesn't mean that you should just brush off the rest of the readings. It means that in those no-instant-click moments, you're going to have to broaden your perspective and think outside your own box. You may be surprised by what you discover.

One or two people in our small group tend to dominate the discussion. Is there any polite way of handling this?

Did you set up ground rules with your group? If not, review the suggestions in the previous section and incorporate them. Then do this: Before each discussion, remind participants that each person's thoughts, insights, concerns, and opinions are important. Note the time you have for your meeting and then dive in.

If this still doesn't help, you may need to speak to the person who has arm-wrestled control. Do so in a loving manner, expressing your sincere concern for what the person is talking about and inviting others to weigh in as well. Please note: A one-person-dominated discussion isn't *always* a bad thing. Your role in a small group is not only to explore and expand your own understanding; it's also to support one another. If someone truly needs more of the floor, give it to him. There will be times when the needs of the one outweigh the needs of the many. Use good judgment and allow extra space when needed. Your time might be next week.

One or two people in our small group rarely say anything. How should we handle this?

Recognize that not everyone will be comfortable sharing. Depending on his background, personality, and comfort level, an individual may rarely say anything at all. There are two things to remember. First, love a person right where he is. This may be one of his first experiences as part of a Bible discussion group. He may be feeling insecure because he doesn't know the Bible as well as other members of the group. He may just be shy or introverted. He may still be sorting out what he believes. Whatever the case, make him feel welcome and loved. Thank him for coming, and if he misses a meeting, call to check up on him. After one of the studies, you may want to ask him what he thought about the discussion. And after a few meetings, you can try to involve him in the discussion by asking everyone in the group to respond to a certain question. Just make sure the question you ask doesn't put anyone on the spot.

During our meeting time, we find ourselves spending so much time catching up with each other — what happened over the previous week — that we don't have enough time for the actual study.

If the friendships within your group grow tight, you may need to establish some time just to hang out and catch up with one another. This is a healthy part of a successful discussion group. You can do this before or after the actual study group time. Some groups prefer to share a meal together before the study, and other groups prefer to stay afterward and munch on snacks. Whatever your group chooses, it's important to have established start and finish times for your group members. That way, the people who are on a tight schedule can know when to show up to catch the main part of the meeting.

At our meetings, there are times when one or two people will become really vulnerable about something they're struggling with or facing. It's an awkward thing for our group to try to handle. What should we do?

This study is designed to encourage group members to get real and be vulnerable. But how your group deals with those vulnerabilities will determine how much deeper your group can go. If a person is sharing something that makes him particularly vulnerable, avoid offering a quick, fix-it answer. Even if you know how to heal deep hurts, cure eating disorders, or overcome depression in one quick answer, hold your tongue. Most people who make themselves vulnerable aren't looking for a quick fix. They want two things: to know they aren't alone and to be supported. If you can identify with their hurt, say so, without one-upping their story with your own. Second, let the person know you'll pray for him, and if the moment is right, go ahead and pray for him right then. If the moment isn't right, then you may want to pray for him at the end of the meeting. Walking through these vulnerable times is tricky business, and it's going to take a lot of prayer and listening to God's leading to get you through.

Some group members don't prepare before our meetings. How can we encourage them to read ahead of time?

It can be frustrating, particularly as a leader, when group members don't read the material; but don't let this discourage you. You can begin each lesson by reading the section together as a group so that everyone is on the same page. And you can gently encourage group members to read during the week. But ultimately, what really matters is that they show up and are growing spiritually alongside you. The REDEFINING LIFE studies aren't about homework; they're about personal spiritual growth, and that takes place in many ways—both inside and outside this book. So if someone's slacking on the outside, it's okay. You have no idea how much he may be growing or being challenged on the inside.

Our group members are having a tough time reaching their goals. What can we do?

First of all, review the goals you've set. Are they realistic? How would you measure a goal of "don't be frustrated at work"? Rewrite the goals until they're bite-sized and reasonable — and reachable. How about "Take an online personality test" or "Make a list of what's good and what's not-so-good about my career choices so I can talk about it with discussion group members" or "Start keeping a prayer journal." Get practical. Get real. And don't forget to marinate everything in lots of prayer.

notes

Lesson 1

1. Reprinted by permission. Donald Miller, *Searching for God Knows What* (Nashville: W Publishing, a division of Thomas Nelson, Inc., 2004), p. 116. All rights reserved.
2. Bill Thrall, Bruce McNicol, and John Lynch, *TrueFaced: Trust God and Others with Who You Really Are* (Colorado Springs, Colo.: NavPress, 2003), pp. 12-14.
3. "One who pretends to be what he is not, one who pretends to be better than he really is, to be virtuous, without really being so," *Webster's New World Dictionary* (New York: Simon & Schuster, 1996).

Lesson 2

1. Ted Roberts, "Healing 'Father Wounds,'" *New Man Magazine*, July/August 2003, http://www.newmanmag.com/a.php?ArticleID=7831.
2. Kenneth L. Woodward, "Hallowed Be Thy Name: Image of God as Father Is Declining," *Newsweek*, June 17, 1996, http://www.highbeam.com/library/doc3.asp?DOCID=1G1:18375188&num=5&ctrlInfo=Round18%3AProd%3ASR%3AResult&ao=&FreePremium=BOTH. All rights reserved. Reprinted by permission.

Lesson 3

1. "I Am Trapped," *Relevant*, n.d., http://www.relevantmagazine.com/life_article.php?id=3536.
2. Jim Thornton, "Take It from Me: Ben Roethlisberger: Steelers QB Ben Roethlisberger Shows You How to Launch Your Own Winning Streak," *Men's Health*, July 26, 2005, http://www.menshealth.com/cda/article.do?site=MensHealth&channel=guy.wisdom&category=life.lessons&conitem=dae25fcb93455010VgnVCM100000cfe793cd____&page=2.

Lesson 4

1. Andy Stanley, *The Next Generation Leader: Five Essentials for Those Who Will Shape the Future* (Sisters, OR: Multnomah, 2003), pp. 55-56.
2. William C. Taylor, "The Leader of the Future: Harvard's Ronald Heifetz Offers a Short Course on the Future of Leadership," *Fast Company*, June 1999, http://www.fastcompany.com/magazine/25/heifetz.html.

Lesson 5

1. Dietrich Bonhoeffer, *Life Together*, trans. John Doberstein (English translation: New York: Harper & Brothers, 1954; copyright renewed: Helen S. Doberstein, 1982), p. 20. Reprinted by permission of HarperCollins Publishers.
2. "Worthy Relationships," *Relevant*, n.d., http://www.relevantmagazine.com/god_article.php?id=5141.

Lesson 6

1. Reprinted by permission. *Captivating*, John and Stasi Eldredge, 2005, Thomas Nelson Inc. Nashville, Tennessee, pp. 6-7. All rights reserved.
2. Nora Ephron, *When Harry Met Sally*, directed by Rob Reiner (Century City, CA: MGM/United Artists Home Entertainment, 1989).

Lesson 7

1. Stephen L. Carter, "Becoming People of Integrity," *The Christian Century*, March 13, 1996, http://www.highbeam.com/library/docfree.asp?DOCID=1G1:18118938&num=7&ctrlInfo=Round18%3AProd%3ASR%3AResult&ao=&FreePremium=BOTH.
2. Nate Penn, "Mr. Dirty Comes Clean: In a Compelling Book, Former NFL Hit Man Bill Romanowski Reveals How He Became Football's Most Feared Player," *GQ*, November 2005, http://men.style.com/gq/features/full?id=content_3969.

Lesson 8

1. Robert J. Samuelson, "Ambition and Its Enemies: A Secret of America's Success, It Both Prods Us to Achievement and Condemns Us to Failure," *Newsweek*, August 23, 1999, http://www.highbeam.com/library/doc3.asp?DOCID=1G1:55474289&num=7&ctrlInfo=Round18%3AProd%3ASR%3AResult&ao=&FreePremium=BOTH. Reprinted with permission.
2. Gordon S. Jackson, comp., *Quotes for the Journey, Wisdom for the Way* (Colorado Springs, Colo.: NavPress, 2000), pp. 150-151.